I Will Not
Be Denied

Written By

Charles A. Dunn

CONTENTS

INTRODUCTION: I WILL NOT BE DENIED

Since the human body is constructed from a position of warehousing a spirit that flows from omnipotence, the spirit itself moves in accordance with that source.

There are laws that govern all events, processes, and agendas. Knowing those laws, their origins, how they work, and why they're in place allows you to bend and manipulate according to your will. This is only a tiny portion of our ability to achieve and accomplish from any vantage point.

Free will and free choice are an inheritance from an energy of duality. We are born to win, but people choose to lose. They lose their mind, their sense of self, and the true sight of life. They study effects instead of bathing in the causes. You worry about what's coming, and the wisdom exists in the energy of the now.

I wrote I WILL NOT BE DENIED because I was summoned to do so from within. Everyone has lost their thirst for victory, but we come from a victorious God. We've divorced discipline and married excuses, but with it, it's until death do us part.

All the advancements of technology have quickened communication travels, but slowed our senses from listening to one another. Every time you use a cell phone without acknowledging the energy that called upon you first, you're crippling your soul phone with your cell phone. We receive and transmit signals of communication to one another. However, we ignore the messages and delay our responses, mainly because we're just not aware that they are, indeed, messages traveling to us.

Then, at those frequent times that we collide with the

one we thought of or who thought of us, we say, "Oh, it's a coincidence, I was just thinking about you..."

Everything we say, do, and believe is making us a nation of underachievers. We're fighting against our own efforts, dreams, and aspirations, even with our words. The proper thing to say when someone calls you while you're thinking about them is, "I see you got my message," or either "I received yours..."

Take the time to figure out who sent the message first. That way, you realize the certain ways that messages are transmitted and received. Without doing so you're training yourself to be reactive and not intuitive. Not being denied is about acting on your intuitions and following your intuitive formulas. Most foods and drinks also help to pull us away from our natural abilities to excel, causing us to become less moody, tired, and erratic. Moderation of certain foods and drinks is important for concentration and goal-obtaining. I could go on and on about endless tools for the true obtaining of goals. I'm not a dream chaser, or a dream maker. More importantly, I am a dreamcatcher.

The majority of society doesn't even dream anymore. Most of the world is following the follower. Without any definite purpose of their own, most of this nation is indoctrinated and not educated. We 've bred a nation of robots that are reacting to a nation full of programs. To see man and woman in their rightful form, you would have to see them when they're very young. Even the ages at which our youth stop dreaming for a better tomorrow are getting younger and younger each year. Without a dream, how can you have hope? Without hope, how do you develop faith and without faith, how can you ever win?

This book is about the details of winning. It's about the mind, heart, and language of a champion. We are all born to champion our lives. Somehow, we are serving the things that were made to serve us. We've reduced ourselves to serving material possessions and becoming emotional slaves to troubled times.

Can you imagine being a creator, and now you're being destroyed by what you created because you forgot that you created It? We know a lot about outer reality, and nothing about inner reality. Thus, what we think we know about outer reality is not true. We know too much about what man and woman have created, and not enough about what created them. We've gotten too far away from the active formulas of their creations. It's like being the user of a clock, and never taking the time to see what makes it tick. When the clock breaks down, you don't know how to fix it because you were only a user of it. We've gotten away from nurturing, and even further away from nature.

I was fortunate enough to be able to realize enough to figure some things out, like how to allow your environment to teach you how to achieve. Through humility and perseverance, you can be almost forced into greatness if you're listening to your inner voice along the way of life. I will not be denied because of God's decree that when we follow certain principles, formulas, and laws that we can't be denied. It's a spiritual inheritance that I've been blessed to be able to recognize, utilize, and that I am still in the process of maximizing.

The information in this book is probably some of the most valuable information that most will ever be exposed to in their lifetime. It's much more than being introduced to concepts that aid you in the advancement of your life.

This book is about the most important part of any information or knowledge. The most important part of any knowledge is how to use it.

I compiled this small amount of information to spark the innate wealth of knowledge in you. It doesn't take a lot of knowledge or information to ignite a positive revolution into an evolution. Each and every one of us are born connected to an endless supply of' all that we could ever need. It's just that most people have forgotten that it is there, and others have forgotten how to use it. I wrote this book to be the flame that ignites the blaze in you.

After you read this book, and if you only remove one of the impediments to the fulfillment of your dreams, then every word that I've put on these pages was worth it. You see, since I can remember, no matter what I faced, the words I spoke were, "I will not be denied." My attitude is the same, and so is my belief in myself. In this material, I'm sharing some of the deepest material put in the simplest terms. Nothing holds power over us but our fears, doubts, and belief systems. That is, until we truly understand that they have no power at all, and we decide to do something about it. I've been through a lot, but I've always felt more powerful than whatever I was going through. You too should feel the same way.

This book will take you into the essence of miracles and the contradictions of impossibilities. It provides simple methods that may aid you in getting past complex problems. There is nothing too large to handle, and nothing too wide to get around in your life.

I believe in God; therefore, I will believe in myself. Everything else is secondary, and we are what's necessary. In order to have a life full of progress that's beneficial, you must be able to see through what is artificial.

"The proper perspective produces a prosperous opportunity."

THE REASONS WHY

One day, many years ago, a wise man once whispered this to me, "Charles, never sell yourself short." I know that we know that we're human beings, but one day, I had a dream about a supernatural being. His capabilities were amazing, and he was given total domination over everyone and everything. He had to be directly handmade by God himself. Let me briefly summarize or highlight some of his supernatural traits. He had five subjective senses:

1. Psychokinesis: the ability to move objects with the mind
2. Telepathy: supposed paranormal communication of thoughts; mental communication
3. ESP: extrasensory perception; ability to read minds
4. Clairvoyance: faculty of perceiving the past
5. Precognition foreknowledge of the supernatural kind: ability to read the future

He had the ability to imagine anything and manifest it without any interruption. His intuitions could pick up bad energy or good energy from anyone upon contact. His immune system was like having a built-in hospital. Any virus or disease didn't stand a chance because his immune system had any medicine known to man, and others not known to man. He had the ability to think himself well or ill. He had millions of tiny breathing holes in his skin that rid the body of toxins while at the same time, taking in nature's natural oxygen.

His capabilities were like no other living organism

created. He had every living being's traits, but none were like him. He could run, jump, spin a web, fly, create a colony, build a nest, hunt, take a life, and save a life. I was amazed at how he could travel the universe in a vehicle much more complex than a spaceship: his mind.

When the old man was finished telling me about this superhero, I began thinking to myself that entire day about all that he said. What I asked myself was, "how did that supernatural being handle intangible?? What was his level of forgiveness? How hard did he love? Was he a great listener? Was he humble? Or was he really arrogant? I can't remember how long after I thought about these questions did that same old wise man come and whisper in my ear again. This is what he said to me:

"You wondered about the supernatural being's intangibles? Let me share this with you. The supernatural being's level of achievement in his physical endeavors will be based upon how in harmony he is with his intangibles, as you call them."

Putting it plainly, the supernatural being wouldn't be such if he didn't adhere to the principles of forgiveness, love, and humility. You see, love that you speak of is not even love in its true form. It is love interrupted, and love tainted by the love itself through the reflection of another. The masses don't acknowledge love until they think they have it for another, or another has it for them. That's love interrupted by the reflection of itself. It's tainted by vanity.

The world will be much better off when they realize that you can't possess love. Love possesses, and it guides you to perpetuate its energies that spring forth from pure consciousness. This is why you must love yourself first.

People say it, but don't come close to understanding the true meaning behind it. Love must not wait for the reflection of it to know of itself. Your life is love manifested. That also is true love consciousness.

When you wait for a reflection or someone to love, they may reflect something other than love, due to the fact that the reflector hasn't loved him or herself first. Or, shall I say acknowledged the love of themselves first. The reflections shouldn't be able to teach the reflector. The reflection is only reflecting. As long as a person keeps pure love consciousness of self, he or she can make it through anything. The world is only reflecting what we feel about ourselves.

And forgiveness? Forgiveness is to give before. The supernatural being understands that forgiveness is to forgive you before you've done your ill or harm. That is why it is called forgiveness. The supernatural being knows these principles intimately from birth, already comprehending that with choice and free will mixed in with carnal desires, plenty of mistakes will be made. Someone may not be perfect, but the life that springs forth from the pure consciousness comes from the concept of perfection.

Humility you speak of, the supernatural being embodies the very expression of humility. Like I mentioned before, he couldn't be a master without humility. Many people hindered their successes and rise to the top by not staying humble. The supernatural being knows that he must decrease to increase. He understands that in order to evolve, he must be able to dissolve in the truth. One must be able to hold what you have, but be humble in order to receive more. Dissolving in the truth is being able to break down your ingredients in order to collaborate with enriched ingredients. Once again, his level of ascension could only be reached due to his submission to his greater supply.

Be mindful of what we 're dealing with here. Everything springs from underlying consciousness. We are speaking about a supernatural being, realizing that he comes from pure consciousness. In the deepest level of reality, consciousness creates creation, so when an entity is in total pure consciousness, they dictate the material world on dominating levels. All of this is housed in a miraculous masterpiece of a vessel.

As complex as all that I've said many appear, the supernatural human body is equally fascinating. His organs, bones, and tissues are predominately made up of four elements: carbon, nitrogen, hydrogen, and oxygen. Also, it's not coincidental that most of the materials in this entire universe are made up of the same materials.

The supernatural being's heart beats approximately 100, 000 times a day, meaning that it beats over 2 billion times a year. It pumps about six quarts of blood through vessels, capillaries, and arteries that stretch out close to 12, 000 miles long, This is why I stated he can think himself well or ill. His heart pumps blood through all the cells in his body. If his thoughts and emotions get out of whack, his body will surely follow. The cells in his body are spying on his thoughts.

The wise old man's words resonated with me. At times, throughout the days that followed, I would catch myself stuck reflecting on his words about the supernatural being. I couldn't help but ponder the fact that nothing and no one could stop the supernatural being from achieving anything. Fearless is the first word that came to mind when I thought about what a supernatural being's mindset should be with all that he possesses. I mean, what other mindset could he have?

The second word that comes to mind is obedience. He had to be obedient to the laws that governed his abilities in order for his abilities to vibrate on that level of productivity.

Wow! I thought to be unlimited in all that you seek to do. To be so unique that all your dreams emerge into your constant reality. All actions and behaviors are fluctuations of consciousness. To come face to face with the blessing of being a supernatural is to never allow your dreams or your desire to dream to be confiscated from you again.

The mere thought of superior human excellence provoked deeper thoughts in me; like, what could I do to perform on much greater levels? Even though I knew I wasn't the supernatural being, that did not have to stop me from being motivated by the fact that one existed.

As it did before, time elapsed and the wise old man whispered to me again.

"You are going to be in a very fortunate position, which is to have the opportunity to recognize the supernatural being and yourself, and to know beyond any shadow of a doubt that there is no difference between you and him. All men are created equal. You have five hundred muscles, two hundred bones, and more than six miles of nerve fibers, exactly as he has. You have thousands and thousands of miles of arteries and veins, which your heart pumps blood through. You both have over twenty thousand fibers in each ear that assist you in hearing. Your body's cells renew themselves every seven years."

None of what he shared with me was as powerful as

him saying, "My dear friend, you are the supernatural being! You are the supernatural being vibrating on a slower vibrational plane. I say that you are he, and he is you. No great prophet or messenger came to tease you with an example of a man that you weren't already. They were all images of who you are from birth. You were born truth and grew up a lie. The secrets of who you are were kept from you. Not from an evil, dominant race. Not from some secret brotherhood seeking to have all the money and power, but from you. No man, fraternity, or race of people can hide God from himself. No matter what comes forth, the consciousness will always surface. Only God could hide him from himself. Thus, I present you to yourself. Like most, you've been playing a very serious game of hide and seek with your supernatural self. While living in a world of fleshly desires, you hide the self that doesn't desire the flesh, but seeks the self that desires nothing else but the flesh. Hence, a supernatural being ends up being controlled and governed by laws of the flesh. Whatever you focus on, you breathe life into. You can't vibrate in greatness when you focus on the ramifications of mediocrity.

The world in its carnal facets is a world of limits. You can only run so fast, jump so high, lift so much weight, stand so tall, or bleed so much. Is that true? Or, is that just more limiting information to help you hide your God self from the lower self? Don't ever take things for what they appear to be, because what appears to be is just that: an appearance.

You appear to be just who gave you your belief system of all that a man is and can do? People read tons of literature that say all these marvelous things about the possibilities of human existence; yet and still, no one believes that. People read all these religious doctrines and it excites them, but it doesn't ignite them. They fellowship and read it, but don' t believe it past the emotional contact of it. It's like watching the World Series, the Super Bowl, the NBA Finals, or any national or world sports competition. There's plenty of excitement, entertainment, emotion and fellowship, but when the function ends, the concentration does as well. It then diminishes to highlighted talk that continues to reduce itself with each passing day.

You can't ascend back to your divine self with mere reading of superficial knowledge. It takes study, concentration, and practice on a consistent basis in order to operate in your supernatural self.

Because it is my personal belief that most come to this plane of things made manifest, descending in order to experience carnal life. To ascertain what is inherently yours, all one must do to begin is spend time alone. Get acquainted with your inner voice. Be attentive and have deliberate action of obedience. Adhere to all that I've said, and more of what you've felt from what I've said. Then, you will truly understand that you and everyone who recognizes what they are have boundless power. You then become unstoppable in this land. You see, nothing in this world can stop a power not from this world.

I do believe that in the Bible verse of John I4: I2, Jesus stated, "The works that I do shall he do also; and greater works than these shall he do." He too was in it, but not of it.

I accepted what the old man said as true. I knew it was true. I felt it. From that moment on, I would realize that acceptance is a very deep power. How high or deep my acceptance was or is would determine how far I could go in walking a greater path. You can never create something in your life that you do not accept. All of what materializes in your life is an accurate reflection of all your acceptances. Your desires fail because you never truly accepted them as truth without doubt. Which is greater, your acceptance of a thing, or your doubt of it? One must crystalize the goals of their life and accept their presence now— without any doubt.

That old wise man that kept whispering in my ear is a prophet of sorts. He resides in me, as yours does you. That consciousness is always untainted, unbridled, and unrestrained. It processes all your experiences, encounters, and information, and then delivers wise counsel. Some people listen and accept, but most don't. Most listen and accept more of everyone else's chatter than their inner voice of reason.

All my many run-ins with all kinds of knowledge on all levels have left me with one realization. The truth connects to you. It confirms itself in past, present, and future experiences. Don't give your power away to authorities, negative experiences, or positive people with limiting beliefs. I know what I am: enough to do what I choose to do in this world, and so can you.

WILL YOU PLEASE GET IT OUT?

Growing up, I was made fun of and picked on for having a speech impediment. I stuttered really badly. I dreaded speaking to anyone, or in front of other children or adults. The strain that I put on my vocal chords from stuttering led to growths, or knots, that had to be surgically removed. My voice was permanently hoarse, and I also couldn't get one word out without stuttering. I was determined to speak correctly and effectively. I heard that still voice inside of me tell me that if I wanted to speak clearly and powerful, that no one or nothing could stop me. I knew that it was part of my birthright from God.

Back when I was young, (and I'm sure it's probably the same today), if a child had any special learning needs, he or she was criticized. Going to a special instructor in a special private room instantly meant you were too special. Well, I had to have that special instructor in that special room because that's where I received speech therapy. I attended speech therapy at Trotwood Junior High School for two days a week, for two years I remember how intense my speech therapy sessions were. When the sessions first began, I was releasing more tears than words. I cried from frustration of not being able to get a word out fluently; cried from the pressure that I felt the therapist was putting on me to incorporate proper speaking methods. At times, I cried because it felt as though my brain was shutting down or locking up.

Nonetheless, through all the tears, the embarrassments, criticisms, frustrations, and pressures, I was determined to turn my speech impediment around. The therapist instructed me on how to slow everything down and drag words out. In hindsight, I realize it was more about slowing down the mind.

Toward the end of the two years of speech therapy, I had the outpatient surgery on my vocal chords. I was told it was relatively simple, but as a child, no surgery is simple when you go in a hospital and you're laid out on an operating table. I was put to sleep for the surgery, and the doctor went in through my mouth and cut the growths off my vocal chords.

Initially, I was told that it was an exploratory surgery to find out why my voice was so hoarse, but upon the doctor uncovering the problem, he corrected it. I was instructed by the doctor not to attempt to speak for a week; basically, the time was needed for healing. I had no problem with that because I wasn't too fond of speaking anyway. To me, speaking went hand in hand with being laughed at. Therefore, I took full advantage of the doctor's request and didn't speak for two weeks.

Growing up, I found my voice by expressing myself through the pen. Writing was something that I became good at, due to my speech problems. When a person is paralyzed in a particular area, they will grow stronger in other areas to overcompensate. A blind individual intensifies their senses of touch, hearing, and smell.

By the time the speech therapy sessions had ended and my vocal chords had healed, a powerful speaker was born. Through the grace of Cod, by the time I entered high school, adults and children would go out of their way to dialogue with me. People would always tell me that I hypnotized a group of people whenever I spoke. I knew that God birthed me with the right to achieve anything that I placed in my heart and was willing to dedicate my energy to.

Now, I am blessed by God and very fortunate that many people say that I'm one of the most powerful speakers that they've ever heard. I humbly say to the world, don't get mad, angry, spiteful, or shameful at anything that anyone says about you. Simply get motivated! Forgive people for what they say against you because it will destroy you if you don't.

Life is less about what happens to you, and more about how you respond to it. No one has control over you. It is you that gives away your power willingly to people's whims, expectations, stereotypes, and views. Nothing that anyone can say to you can make you feel anything. You make yourself feel bad, mad, or sad. When you have an equal choice to smile, laugh, or be glad, you and only you have the choice.

Only change something about yourself when you feel like it needs to be changed. You can't be what others want you to be and be happy with yourself. Nonetheless, when you know something needs to be changed, you owe it to your creator and then yourself to get to it and get it done. Use everything that you once allowed to make you feel inadequate, and let it motivate you to accomplish the goal.

I was fearless, inspired, and relentless about overcoming my speaking impediment. Now, just fearless, inspired, and relentless when I speak.

SKIN I'M IN

Learning to love yourself completely is imperative to true success and fulfillment. I grew up being the darker complexion of all my peers. Absolutely no one that I was around was even remotely as dark as I was. Neither my mother, brother, uncles (on both sides), father, nor any of my grandparents are as dark as I am.

When I examine my thinking about this fact that I discovered as a youth, I think about the origin. I retraced why I even noticed that, and why that fact even took up valuable space in my thinking. Children don't know anything is wrong with race or color, until they are taught. We are born right and taught wrong. I paid attention to my darker skin because it too was made fun of.

When I wore anything black to school, children would tell me that I was naked, and that I better go home and put some clothes on. If I wore a black t-shirt with some sort of logo (in a different color) on it, people made jokes about how I had a tattoo, suggesting once again that I was naked, but that the logo on the t-shirt was actually a tattoo on my chest.

Jokes calling me blue black, midnight, charcoal, and many more insulting names were directed at me in my preteen years. When you combined the speech problem, the big head, and the dark skin complexion, I had to develop a tough resolve to maintain inner peace growing up.

My aunt Ruth, who is my father's sister, sparked me recognizing the beauty of my skin. Unlike anyone else in my family, my aunt was almost as dark as I was, and even today is not too far behind me. Whenever I went to visit her in Detroit, which was many times throughout the year, I noticed how she cared for her skin. I noticed how beautiful and smooth that my aunt's face would always be. I started watching her, and what she did to have those results.

One day, I watched her as she washed, cleansed, and purged her skin of dirt and oils. I couldn't help but notice the many different facial scrubs, creams and products that my aunt had in her personal bathroom. When I questioned her about the purpose of all the products, she would just say, "God gave you beautiful skin, you have to keep it clean and beautiful." She taught me how to give myself a facial and properly care for my skin. She never had to say a word to me about being proud of the skin God gave me to be in. I saw it in the way she cared for her own skin, and how beautiful it was and still is to the date that I'm writing this.

A child may not do everything that adults tell him or her to do, but they will never fail to imitate them. Ever since I could remember, my aunt always received numerous compliments about how beautiful and smooth her skin is. I chose to follow suit with my auntie. I chose to believe in my skin being dark and beautiful, and not dark and ugly. Once again, I couldn't change my skin (like my head), but could keep my skin smooth, clean, and I could believe in my uniqueness.

As I became a teenager, I started to receive compliments about having a smooth skin complexion. I actually had women tell me that I had a beautiful skin complexion before I even graduated from high school. However, none of that happened until I chose to embrace my own individuality and believe I was handsome. When I started caring for myself and my skin like it was important, then it became special to others.

How I was able to handle the criticism as a youth was paramount to the level of tenacity that I go after goals with today. You see, once again, we have to go back to programming. Fear, doubt, and disbelief are the enemies of achievement. These elements are birthed from what negative self-concepts we internalized as children.

Garbage in, always garbage out, and a lack of self-confidence as adults comes from a lack of personal achievement as children. I was blessed to receive a lot of empowering and encouraging energy from God. I rebuked a lot of negative energies growing up that could've ignited a self-condemning spirit in myself. I know that I was born to be above that, and to walk a much different path. Thus, I searched for the silver lining in every situation. My desire was for light, goodness, and moment to moment meaning.

The petty programming that children receive comes from everywhere. Things that most people would never think about influence the thinking of children. Things like driving past dilapidated homes, run down communities, and stripped down cars on bricks every day can negatively begin planting seeds of doubt and lack in a child's mind. A child can witness those things, but they need to also see pictures of complete, whole, and properly functional things as well. They need to see things that are in their original state that God intended for them to be in. For instance, in the projects, you learn to accept dirt and broken glass as being normal for your front yard. Over time, you accept it and start to expect it.

Whenever I traveled to Detroit and revisited my father's side of the family, I would always be in amazement of the well-kept neighborhoods. My aunt

Ruth stayed in Southfield, Michigan, which is like a suburb of Detroit. Her grass was so green and manicured that I adored riding past all of the homes in her neighborhood. No matter where you looked, there wasn't a piece of trash to be found on any of the sidewalks. It didn't matter that I didn't live in those homes. What mattered was that they existed and, as a child, I saw an alternative to beat down neighborhoods. The lawns in Southfield were so nice that I felt uncomfortable walking on the grass.

Even as a child, I can recall how peaceful I felt in that environment. Not to mention, my aunt Ruth and her then boyfriend Bernard (now her husband) always had jazz music playing in their homes and cars. Being in their company always made me feel so relaxed and peaceful. I don't want to fail to mention that the air smelled different in my aunt's neighborhood. My aunt Ruth and Bernard always kept nice smelling air fresheners in their cars, and their homes were also wonderfully scented.

Sounds, smells, and sights will positively or negatively impact a child's thinking. They can make a child care for his or her environment or not. They may take pride in their environment or not.

Whatever the case, it will come down to the individual value system that is instilled in that particular individual. Just because you don't have much doesn't mean that you shouldn't be grateful for what you do have and take pride in caring for it. I don't care if you can't afford to move out of a low-income housing area; you can still put your child on a bus and let them see a better way of living. A person can only go as far as their origin of information. Expose them to more, and they will want more.

I can't even remember a time when my mother

(Joanne Dunn) didn't work a job. We were on food stamps for a very short time period, but my mother refused to sit at home and not work. Also, I can't even remember my grandmother (my mother's mom) ever working a nine to five job. Nonetheless, she was the epitome of a hustler and loaned money to everyone who knew her. When I say my grandmother had money to burn, I mean she had money.

Every day of my life that I saw her or worked with her, she had a purse overflowing with money. I mean, anytime she opened her purse, cash would literally fall out on the floor. Keep in mind she had those big purses that old ladies took to church that looked like overnight bags. When I see Tyler Perry's character, Madea, I often think of my grandmother, Sistrunk. She was a smaller version of that character, but dressed exactly like the character Madea.

Once again, even though my father's side of the family appeared to live in better environments, I watched an unbelievable work ethic from my grandmother. I also watched my mother do any job, and even two jobs to provide for my brother and I.

My grandmother baked and sold cupcakes, German chocolate cakes, pies, dinners, and would stay up all night making personalized quilts, blankets, dresses, hats, and gloves. My younger cousin, Tina, and I were like my grandmother's little helpers. My grandmother would stop at every yard sale and garage sale in the city. She bought some of everything. On the weekends, she would get me and set up shop on the corner of a busy intersection on a vacant lot. There, she would have a bake sale, rummage sale, and a dinner sale all in one. We sold and hustled everything.

Everyone in our neighborhood knew my grandmother. My mother told me that when she was young, my grandmother was the candy lady. I was told that everyone bought candy from my grandmother. When I was really young, I remember that my grandmother had a very successful store called, "Ida's Carry Out". Everyone in the community patronized her carry out. Like I mentioned earlier, a person must show a child more, and show them the way to obtain more. My mother and grandmother, Sistrunk, showed me that you work hard for what you want.

One of the most essential ingredients that I picked up from my mother was her ability to dominate a group of people with personality and spiritual value. My grandmother, Sistrunk, was the people's champ in the community. She provided a service for people and always stayed active in church. My mother and grandmother stayed spiritually grounded in Christianity. Like I've mentioned in my book, "Nothing to Waste in the Wasteland," my mother was instrumental in my exposure to religion.

Since as early as I can remember, my mother always fell asleep reading the Bible. I wanted to know what that book was that she always fell asleep reading. At four years old, I found out what the book was, and my hunger for deeper truths began. While writing this book, I called my mother to share with her how I got a little emotional when I wrote about her mother (Grandmother Sistrunk). My mother then asked me a question, and I decided to close out this section of the book by disclosing what she asked me, and my reply to her.

As a note to the reader, I missed out on the last decade or so of both of my grandmother's lives being incarcerated. My mother's mother (Grandmother Sistrunk) died when I was roughly ten years into this prison sentence. My father's mother (Grandmother Annie Dunn) died after I had been locked up over 19 years. My father's mother gave me more heart to heart communication, and more family values. Grandmother Sistrunk showed me how to go get it; the "it" being anything that my heart desired.

The most amazing part to me was that the Dunns and Sistrunks were raised together in Alabama. My grandfathers (Moses Dunn and Frank Sistrunk) were best friends, creating upbringing relationships between the two families, which eventually gave birth to me. In any child is a host of programs, ideals, and learned behaviors. This is the foundation one must build upon. What the individual took in during the foundational stage will determine the level of significant growth and how they grow.

Now, of course, there is one other critical factor in a child that helps the levels and amounts of growth. That critical factor is the spirit of the child. This topic is almost taboo amongst the masses. People accept or feel comfortable about identifying things that are tangible, but when you go to mentioning different energies and spirits, people feel awkward.

The truth of the matter is that people do have different wills, and you can identify different types of spirits in your children. You may have one child that you rarely have to discipline, and one child you may discipline often. Then, you might have another child whom you just tell that you are disappointed in him or her, and that's all it takes. Instantly, they are genuinely remorseful and eager to make a change. A lot of variables go into a person's foundation; even how they are born. Where they are born and what was happening in the world when they were born goes into their makeup.

Like I mentioned earlier, most don't like to delve into topics of spirituality, planetary alignments, and genetic transmissions. Nonetheless, these elements exist and make up a much deeper part of who we are. The Skin I'm In is simply that: the skin I'm in. I learned to fall in love with me and what God chose to do with me, and I am so appreciative for what I look like. Loving yourself is another vital part to being successful at anything that you do.

The question that my mother asked me was, "Why do you think that you were able to overcome all of the negative criticism without having low self-esteem?"

My reply was, "God blessed me with empowering people around me, and an impervious spirit for an indestructible destiny that is available to all."

SUPER DOME

Not everything can be solved, because everything is not a problem. Some things have to be used as they are because they were made specifically for a purpose. Often times, we are too young in existence to truly understand its meaning. In order to truly get it or comprehend the meaning or purpose for a condition, we must adjust how we judge a particular thing. We all may be born with some part of our physical selves that we don't like because it's not quite like everyone else, or it draws too much attention. However, we must realize that it isn't the condition or bodily part that needs changing; it is our perspective.

As an infant, I had a very large head, and my mother told me that everyone talked about how large my head was, so much so that she made a doctor's appointment to get my head checked out. My mother feared that I had a water head (literally). I don't know the precise term for the condition, but I did meet a nice young man with the condition in Columbus, Ohio. His head grew larger at what appeared to be every week, until he died. From what I was told, you actually have water or fluid in your head that makes it expand. Whatever the case, growing up was pretty grueling for me because not only could I not speak properly, but I had a large head with a skinny body.

I hated crowds because whenever I heard snickering or laughter, I just assumed that I was the focus of their laughter. I was called Super Dome, Head Quarters, Brainiac and when any movie would hit the theaters and anything had a funny-shaped head, I became that as well. When Star Wars came out, I was called Chewbacca

Head, but that was nothing compared to when the box office smash E.T. (Extra Terrestrial) hit cinemas. The movie had a skinny little alien creature with a relatively big, funny-shaped head. I don't have to tell you that everyone joked that the character in the movie was actually me. It was rather difficult for me.

It would 've been one thing if it was simply other children making fun of me, but it was also adults. Usually, a child can depend on the adults to ease some of the embarrassment from the taunting of other children. However, that wasn't the case in my situation. My brother's friends were always making jokes and they were four and five years older. Then, what really crushed me was my mother's friends. My uncle Jimmie (my mother's brother) would make jokes, but he spoke blessings over my head as well. He would always grab the back of my head and say, "boy, you got a big ass head, but when anyone talks about your head, you tell them that's where all your knowledge is." He never made references to my head without mentioning how smart, wise, or knowledgeable that I would be. At the time, his compliments and optimism meant nothing to me because the bottom line was it was yet another joke about my head.

Like stated in the last chapter, I cried a lot on my pillow at night from what I thought the cruel abuse of being talked about. Unlike the speech impediment, there was really no cure, antidote, or solution for my big head because there was actually no problem to be solved. I had to develop a different perspective of my head. I needed to stop basing how I saw my head on a comparison of the heads of others. You will always be bigger, smaller, taller, shorter, lighter or darker when you compare yourself to other people. I had to embrace my uniqueness and develop confidence about being different.

I've met many people who developed defensive mechanisms for their insecurities. Some people joke on everyone first to keep anyone from joking on them. I mean, they turn into funnier comedians than most who would dare talk about their physical misfortune. Other defenses are being overly aggressive in order to intimidate people enough to scare them into not joking on them, or being "push over" nice in the hopes that everyone will like them and not joke on them. There are numerous defenses that people use to attempt to keep others from making fun of them, and I didn't want to use any of those.

I have to honestly thank God for my change of perspective because I seriously know that it came from a deeper place within. I never wanted anyone to feel the way I did, so I definitely wasn't going to joke back on other people. I was determined to take the power back that I had given the individuals who were making fun of me. Somehow, I knew that to use a defense meant that one day, someone could have a greater offensive attack and put me right back in that miserable place. I refused to ever be a victim again.

My mother told me that when she took me to the doctor as an infant, the doctor explained that nothing was wrong with my head. He informed her that my head was larger than most, but smaller than some. He explained that my body would eventually grow into better proportion to my head and not look as disproportionate. Once he made his diagnosis that my head was functioning properly with no dangers apparent, the rest would one day be up to me. It was a process, but I can never recall one time when my mother laughed along with anyone joking about my head. On the contrary, she would just simply say "my baby's head isn't that big. Stop talking about his head!"

Ironically enough, my brother, Dwight, never really made fun of me when we were together and, unlike most brothers, he never tried to humiliate me in front of his friends. There really wasn't any humiliating going on in our household. It was just my mother, brother, and I. We were too busy surviving and trying to find our place in the world to be putting each other down. My brother, Dwight, never put me down and would get upset if I cried about anything or let anyone get to me and make me feel less than them. My brother was four years my senior, and he despised weakness.

No matter what anyone else realized or thought, I had to come to a realization myself. I had to first thank God and count my blessings for being healthy in my head. Forget the size of my head. It was functioning wonderfully. I then chose to buy into my uncle's theory that the size of my head was representative of the amount of my knowledge. Finding peace with what I looked like and being genuinely appreciative of everything about me was important.

At a young age, I realized that any and everyone who joked on others was hiding something themselves. They were hiding something and ashamed of even more. Complete-thinking people don't build themselves up by humiliating others. Unlike my speech problem, there wasn't a therapist or a quick surgery to make the size of my head diminish. It was just my commitment to myself to take away my desire for a smaller head. You see, that desire wasn't my own desire. People needed my head to be like theirs in order to make them feel comfortable, not me.

I conditioned myself to embrace my uniqueness and forgive others for their unfortunate views. I refused to be denied the peace of mind that God birthed me with. I couldn't change my head. The blessing crawled into my life when I spiritually developed enough to know that if I could've changed the size of my head, I wouldn't want to. I was about seven years old when I memorized the Prayer of Serenity.

"God grant me the serenity to accept the things I cannot change, the courage to change the things that I can, and the wisdom to know the difference."

EMOTIONAL IDENTITY

Is Your Child (Inner) Still Running Your Life?

When I examine people's actions from all walks of life, I can't help but to attribute a lot of their responses to their emotional identity. I believe that a lot of how we respond to people and situations comes from that. Who raised you? Did you come from a home of two parents or one? What were the attitudes of the person or persons who raised you? How did they respond to adversity? How did they groom you to handle adversity? What type of emotions did you witness in adults around you when you were growing up? Your emotional memories determine how you react to life experiences. Emotions drive you to excel, overcome obstacles, and bring out your best; they also cause you to doubt yourself and bring out your greatest weaknesses.

I also believe that your spiritual base, your zodiac sign, numerology, and current environmental influences combined, play major roles in how you respond to life's stimuli. Nonetheless, you have the power to choose your responses. None of those previous factors make you helpless or guarantee that you must respond in a certain way. This book is about awareness of the factors that keep you in your own way.

This section of the book is not to give you excuses as to why you have doubt, fear, or don't achieve on certain levels. I'm pretty sure you are already great at doing that all by yourself. Instead, this section is about identifying what may have been some of the hindrances that serve to decrease your level of productivity. That way, you may be able to strengthen your tools, harness your emotions, and stop blocking your own blessings. Whether or not you realize this, most of your responses to life are learned behaviors. Therefore, if you're losing in life, it's because you've been taught to lose. However, we are born winners.

Winning is a mentality, just as losing is. It's a relative perspective that is enhanced by more of the same energy. Are you the type that notices that roses have thorns, or are you the grateful one who appreciates being able to recognize that thorns have roses? I Will Not Be Denied is about seeing that there is a way to make the current appearance of a thing merge into what the desired appearance must be for the victory. Your emotional identity really tells you what you believe you can and cannot do. Recognize that your emotions either motivate you or fail to. Acknowledge that your level of enthusiasm is critical to your ability to see through complex times That simple consistent realization is empowering.

Observe others and analyze the emotions that they attach to things, good and bad. There is so much to be learned about success or being triumphant over things just by watching others. My brother is a fighter, and he fought everything and everyone who came against him. My grandmother on my mother's side was a fighter of people, wrongdoing, and poverty. I can never recall a point when my Grandmother Sistrunk didn't go to church. However, I also can't remember a single time when that same grandmother didn't have money, but she served the community. She served the Lord and hustled her butt off (like I previously mentioned).

As I examine my own life, I can't help but to see my own emotional identity and all that helped to establish it. My mother's strong spiritual base gave me a host of intangible tools to go along with all the others. My grandmother (Annie Dunn) and Aunt Ruth on my father's side were the ones who communicated with me about girls, saving money, and all type of different etiquettes.

There is one key thing that I will share with you about this emotional topic. Know that a person can be in one emotional state to obtain a certain goal, but then move to a more evolved emotional state in order to govern and maintain that accomplishment. Many successful people have lost their hard-earned accomplishments because of spontaneous, reckless, emotional outbursts; things that simply couldn't be undone. Don't let your lows get too low, nor should you let your highs get too high. Stay even-kiltered in the pursuit of your goals. Be enthused, but always stay focused.

Emotional identity can damage or hinder a relationship long before it begins, a relationship that may be very important to your goals or dream. I remember a young man I met from Savannah, Georgia; he and I were locked up together in Elkton Federal Prison. He became like a little brother to me. He was confident and very committed in all that he did. Nonetheless, he was humble to those that were respectful or had something to teach him. One day, I remember seeing a burst of emotion come out of him like no other response that I had witnessed from him. I called myself educating him on the respect of women. At the time, he was only nineteen years old, and this is what he shared with me. He said:

"Big bro, I respect all that you have taught me thus far, but with this topic, I have to stop you. There is nothing that you can tell me about a woman. I have three sisters and a mother. I don't believe in kissing a woman on the lips, and I'll never trust a woman. Let me tell you why. I have watched my sisters lie on the phone to guys, fake tears on the phone to a guy when another guy waits in the driveway, have me lie to the one on the phone while she's upstairs having sex with another. One of my sisters did something so dirty I'll never forget it. One day, I heard one of my sister's screaming, making sex noises with this guy. Then, this new guy she just met pulled up in the driveway. I guess she heard the car from her window because the next thing I knew, they both came running down the steps getting dressed. She pushed the one guy out the back door with some lame excuse. Bro, she barely had her clothes back on when she let the new guy in the front door. Only God knows what she did with her mouth upstairs before the new guy came in, but can you believe she tongued kissed him with the other guy's sex still on her mouth? Then, I watched my oldest sister have a good man, and he is the father of her two children. He went to prison for ten months. Bro, the guy begged my sister to at least bring his kids to see him. She never did, and the prison was only twenty minutes away from where we lived. She messed around the whole time he was gone, and he loved my sister. He took care of her and his children. I used to argue with my sister about how bad she treated him. He would cry on the phone when he would call from jail. I was mad as hell at how she treated him. Then, I was even more upset when he got released from prison and went back to her. Of course, she was begging then."

He went on to share with me that he did have one sister who was a good woman, but it wasn't enough to override what he had witnessed in his other sisters and his mother. It took years of talking to him in order for him to understand that not all women would be like most of the females he was raised up with. Even though he was a very masculine and aggressive young man, I had to let him discover his emotional identity in all of that. You have to investigate your emotional identity and see if it is conducive to where you say you want to go. Everything must be in alignment. Your attitude and emotions about things must all line up. An off-balanced emotional identity will cause you to go backward every time you run into a challenge while getting ahead.

If you come from a household where mom yelled and threw temper tantrums to get everyone's attention in the house, then it's likely that you have that as a part of your emotional identity. Children that grow up in verbally and emotionally abusive households end up verbally and emotionally abusing others. I once read a deep quote from somewhere, and it escapes me where I read it at. It read, "hurt people hurt people. Knowing how to talk to, treat, and respond to people is a tremendous key on the road to success. You can't just say that people must realize that you are who you are and that's the way it's going to be due to the fact that you've been that way your whole life. I can tell you that what is going to happen is you will be right where you are your entire life. Yes, you will probably have some level of success if you have some dominant gift in some field, but I promise you that your success will be minimal compared to what it could be. That also goes for any type of relationship as well.

When a child is raised in a home with:

criticism	they learn to be insecure
jealousy	they learn to conceal and hate
yelling	they learn to yell and be confrontational
fear	they learn to doubt
abuse	they learn to abuse .
love	they learn to forgive
praises	they learn confidence
discipline	they learn structure
spiritual knowledge	they learn about God and self
relationship skills	they learn to keep & value relationships
love and sadness	create jealousy
fear and joy	create curiosity
anger and interest	create passion
intensified anger and interest	can cause hatred
ridicule	creates low self-esteem

No matter what emotional place you are in, center yourself. No matter what emotions are weighing heavy on you, balance yourself. Examine how you feel about things and observe others and their responses to things. You might notice how calm and poised someone was in handling a critical situation, or how recklessly out of control someone was in handling a situation that didn't have to be bad. All of this is a learned emotional behavior and comes from the amygdala, the stored emotional memory bank.

If there's a lot of chaos in your life and your relations with people seem to go south, you might need to take the time to investigate your emotional identity. You need to do it anyway, just so that you know yourself better. In science, your emotions are traced back to your brain. The amygdala is the emotional memory bank of your brain; it commands the limbic system to react according to the things that happen to you based upon the emotional memories it has stored. This will determine how you respond to anything and everything that materializes in your life. How you express those emotional expressions is what constitutes your emotional identity. You must be mindful of that in order to maximize every situation.

Emotions are great servants but can be masters as well. Don't confuse managing your emotions with suppressing your feelings. To manage is to organize, regulate, or be in charge of.

To suppress is to put an end to or prevent from being done. There are serving emotions that you can feel when you say: I Will Not Be Denied!

IS YOUR TREE BEARING FRUIT?

Whether an individual is producing from their efforts or seeing nothing from what they're doing reveals a lot. It always amazes me when I notice that people are questioning if they're doing something correct, or if they have the right formula for what they say they're going after. Others don't have a clue what it is they want from their efforts. People are just doing and being without knowing; similar to the behavior of a robot.

The telltale sign that what you're doing or striving to do is right is whether your tree is bearing fruit; your fruit being the production of good results that impact your life and others in a positive way. If a person goes and unstops someone's toilet and then assists another person who needs help with theirs as well, his efforts bear fruit. The mere fact that someone whom the individual assisted referred someone else to that person is fruit. Now, if one of those people who had their toilet fixed referred a third customer to the toilet fixer and he was unable to fix it, his tree is still bearing fruit.

What takes the act to the next level is integrity; basically, how the fixer handles the situation when he is unable to fix the toilet. If the person calls around and at least finds someone else that can fix the toilet, the customer is still satisfied. The customer will probably still call the first fixer before the second fixer because the person saw the project through to the end. Doing the little extras is a good way to produce more fruit.

Most people are satisfied doing a less than stellar or average job. Even in relationships, I've seen so many people self-destruct in their relationships, not owning what they've done and what's needed to correct the problem. An individual might verbally abuse a friend, spouse, or other family member. Justifying their wrong or abrasive actions, the abuser might say, I'm just too real for people... people just can't handle how real I am... I just don't sugarcoat things..." etc. If the way you speak to people creates more problems than solving them, you probably need to fix it. You must always speak the language of the audience. If you're speaking thick Latin language and you're currently in the heart of Jamaica, then it's going to be difficult to convey an understood word; therefore, your words will not bear fruit.

For those who have problems understanding anything outside of sex, I will give you another example. If you think you are the answer to everyone's sexual fantasy, but your efforts with one particular person fall short, you need to alter your approach to sex with that person, or in general.

I can remember being in college and really thinking I was pleasing a girlfriend at the time with kisses one day. She had the courage to stop me and say, "Baby, what are you doing?' Of course, I was speechless and embarrassed by her stopping me, but my efforts to please her were not bearing fruit. The details of what she showed me about pleasing a woman are not for this book! I don't know if you're grown enough for that material. That material must have parental guidance stickers on it. However, the point is that I needed to be shown how to please her so that my intimacy efforts would bear fruit.

Many people are different and require a mixture of things to please them. Thus, you must always realize that if your tree in that field is not bearing fruit, you need to readjust some things. A goal is a goal. It doesn't make a difference if you're going after a climax from your spouse, new position at your job, a certain amount of money, better relationships, better grades in school, or improvement in the realm of sports; your tree of efforts must bear fruit.

The formula for success remains relatively the same, no matter what you're going after. There are elements that must be present in order for the tree of your efforts to bear fruit. The seeds must be healthy for the tree's roots to sprout out. The soil must be rich and pure. The surroundings of the tree can infiltrate the process of the natural elements needed for the tree to grow. Like a rose, toxic and weedy surroundings will choke the life out of a rose. It's a living organism. Therefore, water, sunshine, oxygen, and adaptable temperatures are essential to a tree bearing fruit. Nature teaches us how to prosper if we only take the time to receive the education.

With nature as it is with us, there is an unwavering formula to harvest. There are elements to success, and then there is a natural alignment to those elements. They must fall within their natural sequence. Do not keep doing the same thing over and over and expect different results. That type of behavior negates success or the accomplishment of goals. I make sure that my tree of effort bears fruit. If it doesn't produce something toward the objective for myself or others, then it needs to be altered.

Many people have expended so much energy doing what didn't matter that by the time they figured out what did matter, their enthusiasm was already in a casket being prayed over. I remember, I was failing badly during my first year of college at Columbus State. I had simply been doing too much partying and not studying. I can't really remember if midterms were coming up or if it was finals.

Whatever the case was, I had taken poor notes in my classes, if any at all. None of my closest friends were in any of the classes that I was failing. Therefore, I didn't feel comfortable asking any of the other students for their notes. Plus, I had procrastinated so long that exams were only a few days away, making it extremely difficult to cram three or four different classes of notes into three days.

I followed my past formula of success. I knew that anything I chose to do had to be in furtherance of learning the material in those classes. The first thing I did was calm myself down, told myself that I could pass those exams, then told myself not to panic. I had to open myself to receive the most effective way to go about the goal. I set the books for each class in front of me. and looked at them, visualizing myself passing the exams, then I took a walk outside to release my thoughts. What I didn't explain earlier in this testimonial is that I was doing so badly in two of the courses that the professor told me I would need to ace the final in order to get a passing grade.

After taking a short walk to the corner store and back, the solution came to me when walked back into my apartment. I entered the apartment and walked up to my kitchen counter that books for each class on it. Upon the first glance, the answer was clear. I would simply memorize the glossary. Each effort that I would expend on memorizing a term or word would bear fruit. One word known that was once before unknown would bring me closer to passing the exam. For three days, day and night, I memorized the glossary from the books for the three courses I was failing. I had my then-girlfriend write out flash cards of words, terms, and their definitions. She would drill me.

The end result was confirmation to me about the formula of success. I received a 96% on one exam, and 98% on the other two exams. My instructors were extremely surprised at my scores. They probably wanted to accuse me of cheating, but they knew that I hadn't. They watched us too closely.

No matter what goals you embark on, make sure your efforts bear fruit, moment by moment. Like I've stated previously in my other written material, "there is no such thing as a small accomplishment; just stay in motion. It was only a single rain drop that started the ocean.

UNIVERSAL LAW

Universal Law is the only real law that there is, and it is the intervention of total domination of the dark side. U—law was made as a tool for God to govern himself in human form. It actually prevents the God spirit from making a devil out of himself. That may sound confusing, but this isn't the book to explain the beginning of it all.

U—law is a pure heart's best friend, and a deceitful heart's nightmare. The law shows you a reflection of your own image. It also creates a snowball effect from your past into your present and future. People reference its concept with a lot of different phrases ... reap what you sow... what goes around comes around... and do unto others as you would have them do unto you.

The law even governs living organisms. If you plant apple seeds in the soil, you can't receive oranges at harvest time. The seeds only produce the fruits of its own kind. If we could only understand that this concept governs life and humanity in its entirety, we could walk the earth as gods and goddesses. Every deed that is committed is a seed planted in this lawn.

The law prevails, no matter the situation. It doesn't matter if you recognize it or acknowledge it; it still exists. So much of society is totally oblivious to this law, but yet it governs everything.

Making a conscious effort to act with the highest degree of integrity within this law is a very important key to my success. One must stay in accord with the laws of purity and wholesome living. To cause unwarranted strain to an innocent man is to harm a hair on your own head. To criticize another in public is to ignite the mockery of your own actions in the future.

The chickens do come home to roost, and this is what we all must understand. I, myself, have become consciously one with this law in the understanding of its functions. There isn't any natural law outside of man or woman, and there is no man or woman outside of natural law. The law is not one dimensional, and it does affect the roads that we travel. We create our tears and smiles long before they appear on our faces. We create monsters in our lives and then refuse to claim them.

Universal Law holds your future accountable for the actions of your past. We build these monsters with our thoughts and actions. We cultivate that negative energy, until it explodes into our future. A person must be mindful of what seeds they are planting, Even the street hustlers, ballers, and players have a name for this law. They call it the game code. "Be true to the game, and the game will be true to you," is what they say. That is a statement that was often heard in the street, but seldom followed.

Too many people underestimate this law. It sneaks up on you like a virus creeping through your bloodstream. You're not aware of its presence until it takes control of your current condition. Laws must govern all events. This law has many dimensions and affects every aspect of a person's life. Careful decision-making can instruct and direct this law. A person must think before acting upon a situation. Time may heal physical wounds and only leave a scar. However, it can't heal a negative seed that's been planted in fertile soil. The surface hides the impact of this law, but the perceptive individual can always tell when the law has left a stain on someone's brain, meaning that the soul is in constant turmoil and there's no peace.

For example: the hardest thing about doing serious bodily harm to someone is sleeping with what you've done. When you rest at night, you'll replay it, contemplating if the situation had to escalate to that level or be dealt with in drastic measures. When an individual takes another person's life without just cause, homicide is often followed by a slower suicide, meaning that the situation often haunts senseless murder.

Living with yourself is always the greatest part of decision-making. We can't escape the realities that we create for ourselves. There is no escaping the universal law. The wise individual is able to think hard, heavy, and quick. Know yourself, and don't put a stopwatch on an important decision— make the decision. <u>Think deeply in a crucial moment of your life, or you'll possibly be thinking about that moment for the rest of your life.</u>

One thing that truly bothers me is that men and women alike feel they can lie or withhold things and still get unity and trust out of a relationship. There are no secrets in the universe. People seem to think that they can rob, steal, deceive, and betray people all the way into their fortune. You can't! There's a law that governs all events, and it mirrors the intentions behind your actions as well as your actions themselves. It then projects that reflection into your future.

To not be denied in obtaining goals is to stay in harmony with that law. Treat people right and be of high moral standing in all that you do— even when no one is looking.

All must line up in bringing you the desires of your heart. What you see is initiated by what you don't see, so plant great seeds.

I'M BORED

In most dictionaries, the word bored means dull, weary, repetitive, and uninterested. In most dictionaries, life is defined as the property or quality of living; distinguishing living organisms from dead organisms and inanimate matter; an element that has growth, reproduction and responds to stimuli.

In knowing these two truths, it is in my opinion that a person shouldn't ever be bored, unless they know everything there is to know in life. Living is a direct contradiction with being bored. I honestly believe that one of the reasons for a spirit partaking on the journey of a human experience is spiritual boredom, for a lack of a better word. There's a desire to simply experience life. Joy and pain are equally a part of that experience. At times, we are shaped by what we do. If we do nothing and survive nothing, then ultimately, we are nothing.

So much plagues our lives, and we allow nothing to negatively impact everything. Managing your time and resources wisely is the nucleus to acquiring desired results.

Too much time is wasted on eating, sleeping, and idle chit chat. Most people who find themselves in these rut-driven activities also claim high levels of boredom. Controlled enthusiasm toward a goal is always a guarantee to move through barriers. I have always felt that to say that you are bored is to disrespect the life that you have been granted. To say that you are bored is to take all the possibilities and your possible interactions with them for granted. How can you seek to live, walk, eat, see, talk, imagine, smell, touch, and process those findings and be bored? How can you be bored, but capable of walking outside and feeling the hot, beautiful rays of the sun beat down on your face? Do you know what a marvel just the sun itself is? How the energy off the sun never goes out and what would happen if it did? Did you go outside and just feed a few ants a popsicle stick with a little popsicle juice still on it?

Have you ever witnessed how fast ants can build an ant hill? Have you ever appreciated the patience and vision of a hawk? Watching how it is a hundred feet up in the air circling but can see a mouse the size of your big toe moving in the grass? Grass that might stand halfway up to your knees? You just watched him because you really don't realize what he sees until he swoops down and snatches it up into the air.

Do you understand how powerful the presence of the moon is? Do you understand the power that the moon has on a woman's menstruation cycle? Did you know that the moon is like a woman that's been through menopause?

The moon is like a non-reproductive part of the planet Earth. It can't produce life anymore because it can't hold water, which is the essence of life. This is why Earth is called Mother Earth, or the nature on Earth is called Mother Nature. She reproduces life naturally.

Did you ever pay attention to why you can go to the beach when the sun is out and the water is calm and low, but as soon as the evening comes, the waters get wild? Do you understand why there is high tide on the beach? When you're on the beach and your towel is close to the water when the sun is out, do you have to move it the later it gets? What if I was to tell you that the moon is disrupting the calmness of the water? Would you believe me? Is it the truth? Did you know that the waters are disrupted because the moon is craving for and pulling the water from Earth? Almost like the moon is the mother that has been through menopause craving for her daughter or the life (water) that flows through her daughter? Is this the truth, or something that I made up? What about the hundreds of thousands of people all over the world who are, at this very moment, on their deathbeds?

How many of them do you think would love to be able to live one more healthy, mobile day in order to witness, experience, and investigate all the things I previously mentioned in this chapter? But you're bored, huh? Did you know that you have a lot of hidden forces to discover within yourself?

You have a natural human energy system. You have chakras, or energy conductors, that are like filtration systems. They are whirlwinds of moving energy. They stimulate various organs in the body and release hormones into the bloodstream. Certain hormones affect and control your body, not to mention your state of mind. When we have just a little bit of the incredible knowledge about our incredible selves, we can become more deliberate and intentional with our actions on the paths we choose.

One day, in the cold winter of 1991, I was delightfully stuck in my suburban home in Columbus, Ohio— I say was delightfully stuck because I was with a very beautiful young lady. who came over to spend the evening and the night with me. All that day before I picked her up, I was being tortured by a wisdom tooth that was erupting in back of my mouth. For some strange reason (could it be the moon again), it always seems like toothaches get worse in the late evening and at night. Keep in mind that I was twenty-three years of age at the time, and in my house with a super gorgeous woman who had a body like a goddess. There was no possible way that any young man wouldn't block out the pain for that night.

Well, right when we started to get comfortable in front of my fireplace, my toothache became unbearable. When I say unbearable, I'm talking about eyes turned red, head felt like it was going to explode, and my ears started throbbing. We were having a very deep and spiritual conversation with only the light from the fireplace and jazz music (Grover Washington, Jr.) playing. The mood was set, but my toothache caused too much pain. I finally went in the bathroom to check it out. The gums in the back of my mouth were swollen around the tooth, and a splitting headache also emerged. Suddenly, I had an epiphany. Even though I had not been formally trained on meditation, chakras, and healing chants for the body, I decided to try something. By the way, I had taken aspirin all day. I said they may be life savers, but they did absolutely nothing for the pain.

I actually stood up, gyrating my body up and down, making several noises that I hoped would release the pain. I made the "ohm" sound, as well as others that felt natural to me. I really just went with the vibration of my inner rhythms. I let my body do what came natural to it. Not even five minutes had passed before that unbearable pain stopped permanently and did not return. Of course, I went on and had a wonderful evening.

There is so much to learn about our bodies and the forces within that it would take ten lifetimes to know. However, we have this one we are living now to find, discover, and maximize potential forces and abilities inside ourselves. But you bored, huh?

Growing up, the elders would always say that an idle mind is the devil's workshop. I feel as though the life source is energy in motion. To be in physical form consciousness is to be in motion, creating an agenda and accomplishing it. That's part of the experience. Even to be still, but yet to be visualizing, creating, or willing into existence is still living. However, to embrace a thought of being bored and to attach the words and emotions that come with it is to move closer to a state of death.

I don't necessarily agree with the words staying busy either. As far as replacing the concept of boredom, in my opinion, that is adopting the concept of passing time. You mean to tell me that your current life is but a blink of an eye, and you have time to just pass doing anything? No! Make each moment mean something. Make each moment relevant toward a purpose, a life, a dream,.

To me, being bored is a direct showing of a lack of gratitude for life and what you are capable of. It is also a direct misuse of time and consciousness of the timing of the universe. To be successful in this world, you must make excellent use of your time and when you run out of it, find a way to get some more. When your ultimate cord of a life is cut by the ultimate timekeeper, I believe you'll have plenty of time to be bored again.

IMAGINE THAT

What does your goal look, feel, taste, walk, talk, sound, and smell like? What emotions does it invoke? There is a great power that thought the universe into expression. That power serves those of us who believe in it and confidently use it. The one thing that we must do is supply a clear mental picture of the desired end result of our goals to the universe. Your imagined finished product is your vow of what you shall one day be. It is a representation of your philosophy about where you are headed. Your level of intensity, concentration, and focus is necessary in order to see this through.

Writing what it is you hope to accomplish should never be overlooked. There's a creative magic within expressing a finished victory before the race ever begins. It can be spoken on, written about, or visualized. To truly materialize a goal that has yet to be acknowledged in the land of the seen, it has to be birthed in the heart of the unseen.

The process is:

- Visualize it
- Verbalize it
- Internalize it until it materializes

Create what victory already looks like in your mind. Speak on it decisively and powerfully. Write it down; not the want, but the finished product. Internalize it until it materializes. Sometimes, the best way to start is to write out the success. Other times, the best way may feel like simply visualizing it. I can honestly say that up until the very moment I wrote these words, this process has never failed me. In all honesty, I can say that I've achieved every single major goal in my life that I've applied these principles to.

The first step toward success is developing the process of rehearsal for success. Success has to be rehearsed first. A vision is a great manifestation of creative imagination. It brings forth a strong sense of mission. It fuels human action. A vision goes beyond your current reality, and it creates what appears not to exist. So much of what people have not accomplished in their lives has made them cynical toward the future. We are to live out of our imaginations, not out of our memories.

A powerful vision can be a very motivating force toward the future. Seeing beyond a current undesirable condition is a blessing within itself. Most people get stuck right in the middle of a challenging mess. 'They lay in it, roll around in it, and begin covering themselves in it. They grow an affinity for it, like a pig in slop.

You see, the majority of the world is living from scripts. They spend more time emotionally discussing a problem than visualizing the end of it. Count how many times you share a financial woe or strain in one day. Now, how many times did you create a clear vision of the receipt with that same financial strained paid? I mean, see it to the point where you can see the date on the receipt and watch the ink dry; not to mention, to smell the scent of the paper that the receipt is made of. Not many people know that a vision transforms and transcends.

How many other living organisms do you think have an imagination? What other living beings have the ability to transport themselves to see another place across the planet, while physically never moving? What creature besides humanity has the ability to create moods and feelings from an imagined reality?

Now, I ask a serious question. How many of us in the world really use our imaginations? Out of the few that use it, how many know how to use it properly and maximize its usage?

When focused on a goal, an imagination should never be used to drift away from the goal. While working on important goals, a lot of people's imaginations sense as drifting mechanisms. You must train yourself to have a passionate vision from your imagination or stay in the moment. It's like a pilot flying a plane. Most of the time that he's flying, he's actually getting back on course. Keep that imagination steady, and it will allow you to take yourself so deep into where you are headed that you forget where you are.

The passion from a good, clear vision can literally transcend doubt, discouragement and fear. Like I've mentioned in previous chapters, you are fighting scripts, theories, and emotional identities that encouraged you and trained you to doubt, fear, and disbelieve.

This next part that I shall write about may, at first glance, read as a contradiction to focus and concentration, but it's not. This is the next level to vision, imagination, concentration, and focus. The graduation is letting go.

I've read scores of self-help books that stress the importance of focus and concentration, but none that I've read stress the importance of letting the focus and concentration go. Focus with emotion and action will plow through the distractions and obstacles of life. Your intuitive powers will also be ignited on a more concentrated level and will help you solve problems beyond your daily reasoning. This is an important key to the "I Will Not Be Denied" mentality, but it is not the only key. The key that is equally as important as the focus, concentration, emotion, and action as "letting go."

Knowing when to let it go is most essential to pulling the substance being desired and pursued out of the universe. Knowing when to let go should not be misconstrued with giving up. This intent behind this version of letting go is faith that it is on the way, and not the doubt or discouragement that it is not coming. The one curse that focus and concentration can have is they can shift into worry and doubt over a period of time. How many times in your life have you focused and concentrated on finding something and couldn't until you walked away and came back? How many times have you struggled to solve a problem to the point of frustration, only to release that problem, focus on something else, and when you returned to the original problem, the answer appeared?

Sometimes, you can look for something so hard that you miss it. It's because your sight of a thing is blocked by the act of looking for it. The peaceful mind stops the hard look for a thing in the faith that they will see it. It's a little different, but acquiring something from the desires of your heart has a similar system. The focus, concentration, and action can often lead some people into trepidation or fear when they don't see results in their desired timeframe when, in actuality, one of two things could be happening:

- The person's desired results are already in route to them.
- The signal was never really released into the

universe in order for the request to be fulfilled.

Either way, you are blocking signals by doubting, fearing, or worrying and requesting more of the same. There's a magical draw of your dreams coming back to you fulfilled when you understand how to let it go.

Even though I have been away from technology a long time, I have noticed a supportive example in my theory in a piece of technology: a touch screen smartphone. The way to get the phone to respond directly and correctly to you is to simply tap the command on the phone. If you touch it too hard or hold it too long, what does it do? Well, it immediately perceives a prolonged touch, press or hold as a delete command. If you are trying to dial a phone number or enlarge a picture or anything, you must tap it and "let it go." In that brief concentrated moment, you are basically letting the phone know that are aware it has received the command or the request. To hold your finger down on the phone is to send a mixed signal to the brain of the phone, thus crystallizing my theory's example.

I'm fully aware that this part of the writing in this book could be the trickiest material entailed. Yes, you must focus, concentrate, and hold a clear mental picture of your goal in your mind. Nonetheless, you also must discover the times to let it go.

In my travels and self-discoveries, I 've learned and developed some marvelous tools. I am sure that at first read, a few of the readers might be slightly confused, but read it with your heart you'll get it. We are all born supernatural beings with unbelievable depths of logic. We just know things sometimes and are not really sure how we know. Don't fight the inner knower; just let It flow. You can hold your vision of your completed image at night before you go to sleep, but then let it go and go to sleep. You may see your visualized goal in the morning while you're eating breakfast. Create a smell to go with the vision. If possible, smell it, and smell it heavily!

Next, pull out the tablet and write the accomplished goal on paper. Then, let it all go in your mind instantly and focus on what you're wearing for the day. Next, go get dressed. The letting go of a vision from time to time is an energy assembly of faith; faith that the universe has just issued you a routing number or date when your request will physically appear in your life. Please figure out what I'm saying, because it's simple.

When you fail to walk in this process, you simply hold your wish button down too long on your universal smartphone, thus sending all of your wishes and desires to the delete mechanism or to the garbage can. I will cease being facetious when I write this. One must be careful in wanting something and follow the creative process correctly. You see, most people send out the signals of wanting something to the universe, But most have a self-defeating materialization process of what they say they want. The process that is often used by people in wanting something is received by the universe that they simply want to be wanting it.

To put it plainly, you will never receive what it is you truly desire if you don't create the vision. Speak it, feel it, and see the goal accomplished; then, you must let it go. Do all this daily and repetitiously. Your spirit will tell you when. Get the picture? Imagine that!

GET LOADED

Much of one's genius or cleverness in being triumphant in any endeavor is largely due to preparation. Being prepared for what's to come can be difficult when you have no idea of what is coming. We are born with a very high sense of adaptability. We are capable of transforming our thoughts, emotions, and actions to conform with any path needed. One must realize that most of the aspirations we have end up being like a war of sorts. The war is between the routine of what you've been doing, versus what you're trying to do.

The war is also between the people around you, loving where you are, and not liking where you are going. Family and friends may openly portray that they are supporting you while secretly, inside their heart, they are cheering for your failure.

Beneath it all, they don't want to share you with your success. They care more about the time you spend with them and the things you do for them than seeing you fulfill the pursuits of your happiness. They don't want their comfort zone threatened or disrupted. Rare is the person who loves someone enough to welcome themselves being left behind in the interest of their loved one getting ahead.

Many battles will emerge on a person's journey to accomplish their goals. There is no possible way to foresee all that lurks behind the variations of circumstances and energies. There is no way to see them, but rest assured that the hurdles, resistance, distractions, interruptions, and roadblocks are coming; be it those come from actual people or simply unseen natural challenges. Whatever the cause, they will appear, but they don't have to slow you down or derail your efforts. That is purely your choice.

One of the best ways to keep yourself impervious to the appearance of impediments is to get loaded and stay loaded while on your journey to success. You must not allow things to hinder you or simply drain your energy. Before you go on a trip, what must you do? Surely, you must prepare for the trip. You load up on the things that you know you need or could possibly need. If it's a road trip, you'll make sure you have a spare tire and some type of emergency money or roadside assistance; these are needed just in case some traveling ailment befalls your vehicle. You will pack up clothes, hygiene items, and possibly emergency food and water. When you get it all together, you load it all up and get ready to make the journey.

There is a certain precariousness that comes with any journey or road trip. Well, that's the kind of war taking place. The war is against your dreams and goals. It's against you reaching your destination. The label "war" may seem a bit over the top or dramatic, but it isn't. It is appropriate because we don't take seriously the fact that due to some of the things that get in our way on our journey, most people don't make it. We take interruptions and distractions much too lightly on a life-changing course. You must take the position that whatever is attempting to get in your way is trying to kill you. No, it may not be killing you physically, but it's killing a dream. It's killing a sense of accomplishment, aspirations, and possibly financial rewards for your family. If nothing else, an obstruction in the way to your goals is attempting to kill your God given inheritance to reach those goals. Once you destroy or kill everything inside a person's life, what good is their actual life anymore? Therefore, an individual must take every obstacle and distraction deathly serious. That way, you ignore it, push through it, or solve it with the urgent attention of your life depending on it.

Most successful or goal-oriented people have zero tolerance for being disturbed when they're working on a project. Often times, it may not be an actual person disrupting your mojo on your journey to a goal. It may be a financial woe, a health issue, family crisis, legal problem, and the list goes on. To overcome these issues, they must be defeated before they appear. In the book The Art of War by Sun Tzu, he mentions that the strategy of an individual must be to do what will be hard while it is still easy. Another pearl of wisdom that I've always heard is "Always train for war in a time of peace." I can't remember where I learned that from.

The message in these phrases is this: you must be prepared, and prepared well, for what you may face. You will not get far on your journey if you haven't brought your tools along in order to help you go the distance. The term that I use to name this chapter is what anyone that is pursuing a goal must do. "Get Loaded" is about arming yourself with the weapons to plow through whatever may get in your way on the road to wherever you're choosing to go. For some people, quoting a few Bible verses at night might work. In my opinion, it might take a little more than that for most. That will be based upon the amount of inspiration, focus, passion, and emotion that you attach to whatever information you take in.

I started "Getting Loaded" on encouraging words when I first began to read as a little boy. I've always had an affinity for poignant material. I am loaded on inspirational quotes, poems, bible verses, and wisdom from great philosophers. I'm addicted to well put together sayings that tell you to keep on going, including poems like "Don't Quit" (author unknown), Rudyard Kipling's poem "If," W. E. Henley's poem, "Invictus." I have not only memorized them, but eternalized them and many more. Quotes like, "tough times never last, but tough people do," "the harder the battle, the sweeter the victory," "if you can no longer run, then walk; if you can't walk, then crawl but, by all means, just keep going," I can't remember where I first read those quotes, but those and many more have helped push me through too many victories.

Through decades of challenges and overcoming them, I've developed my own little system. The Bible verse "to whom much is given, much is required" instantly serves as an energizer for me. However, the fact that the verse exists in the Bible isn't good enough to help you. Its message must be reverberating in you. It must almost become a part of your emotional and psychological DNA. One must repetitiously load themselves up with information that encourages, motivates, inspires, and uplifts. Whenever you meet the stumbling blocks, roadblocks, and detours of life, what will you draw from in order to keep on goings?

Every energy surge has a supplier. Every boost of energy has a source. A journey to your goals has many disappointments, let downs, illusions, and frustrations. These elements zap your personal energy supply. Tons of people were at the threshold of victory when they simply ran out of gas (energy, hope, etc.), which brings me to another of my favorite quotes. This one is by Winston Churchill. He states, "when you find yourself going through tough times, just keep on going."

I am not reading these quotes off a sheet of paper as I'm writing this chapter. They just appear as I speak or write. This comes from a lifetime of loading myself with empowering material and staying loaded. Many marvel at how I rattle off hundreds of quotes when I speak without reading from a cheat sheet. With most of the quotes, I can tell you who wrote them and where I get them from.

Getting loaded can also be a particular song that inspires you or ignites you. I definitely feel like you need to be tapped into that higher part of yourself. Once tapped in, you need to feed that part of yourself and keep it going. Getting loaded is building up your spiritual arsenal, as the military calls it. It's also putting on the armor of God, as the Bible explains it. However you choose to explain it, you cannot go into battle unprepared, or you will lose. You cannot go the distance without the mental, emotional, and spiritual fuel to do so.

My mother was diagnosed with breast cancer about seven years ago. From the very beginning, she told me that she was going to fight and defeat it. I too was in agreement. During our fight with cancer, I discovered truths that I would have never believed. A lot of people refuse the full treatment of cancer from the doctor. I mean, tons of men and women refuse the chemotherapy. Due to the side effects of certain treatments, people do not want to journey down that road. Yes, my mom beat cancer after surgery and a host of treatments. Due to her faith, fortitude, and willingness to go the distance, she prevailed.

Cancer is a very serious game changer, and it ends your life quickly. You have to be "loaded up" when you go to war against cancer. My mother would go to sleep reading the Bible every night. She went to church fellowship a couple nights a week, and she stayed prayed up and loaded up. My mother always tells me that I helped pull her through that rough time. Even though I was incarcerated in federal prison at the time, I continuously called her and kept her encouraged. Just calling helps a lot, but when you're giving your mother faith talks and discussing a warrior's walk, you're feeding her spirit to make it.

To read stories of impossible odds and how people overcome those odds is to load yourself up with their fuel. Another way to arm yourself or load yourself with fuel to succeed is with a vision board. Cut out images from an old magazine that fit your end game picture. Put a collage together that accurately depicts what your goals look like already accomplished. Have you ever seen (in real life, or on television) a miniature prototype of a multimillion dollar building that someone is about to build? Most of the time, you can catch them on movies where in the board meeting, the prototype is sprawled across some enormous table. When you do see the miniature display, it is extremely detailed. I mean, they have the mock landscape, street lights, sidewalks and everything. It is an exact replica of precisely what they're going to build. My point to all this is very simple. When you're going after anything in life, you must be loaded up for the journey to it. You must have a clear picture of what your finished product should look like. Even equally important, you need a supply of motivating energy to get you there.

Something inspires you to act. Something sparks you to discover. Something encourages you to keep on going through frustrations. You have to find what that something is and get full on it. Keep a supply of it around you. Keep people around you who motivate you to go after what you want. If possible, when you create your vision board, look at it daily. Burn that picture into your subconscious. Sit at the table in that image. Smell the scent of the wood. Get loaded on what is going to get you there. I love great philosophy books and powerful quotations. There are so many powerful fables, biblical stories, religious stories of faith, and encouraging one-liners that you should never be short on encouragement. Get your mental and spiritual archives loaded up— that's the secret to pushing through the roughest times.

How abundant are your spiritual resources? Every single time something comes against me, at least ten different things come to mind to defeat it. If it doesn't immediately come to me, I just sit still for a moment. God eventually delivers the antidote because I was loaded with the faith that he would.

SPEAKING IT: SELF-TALK

One of the most undervalued, yet most potentially powerful tools that we possess is the power of speech. Many people that do recognize there is power in your choice of words still don't know what to say and what not to say. Words and the emotions that we attach to them have significant influence on your body and the materialization of things in your life.

The words you speak are a power that is in direct accord with your own conscious power. As you develop your level of consciousness, you too should develop the proper way to use the proper words to bring the desired results in your life. We have desires in our heart that are directly contradicted by what we say and what we believe we deserve or can have. Of course, there is no superpower in one word being spoken, nor do I want you to be so afraid of saying the wrong words that you say absolutely nothing. However, I must admit that at times, it would benefit your cause a lot more to simply say nothing. You see, people often plant the seeds in thought and uproot them in breath. Take a moment to read the statements below:

- "knowing my luck, I would get..."
- "if that doesn't happen for me, I'll do..."
- "then again, that's not realistic..."
- "he/she will probably never do that for me..."
- "that's too hard..."
- "that's impossible..."
- "hopefully, I'll get lucky..."

When you speak statements like these, you are

uprooting your seeds of success. There is nothing more empowering or more self—defeating than the power of speech. We speak but fail to comprehend the power of speech. We constantly do one thing, desire another, and speak something totally different. We cannot get the desires of our heart if we fail to speak the languages of manifestation. Everything and everyone has a language that speaks correctly and directly to the essence of itself. There's languages of defeat, misery, lack, love, confidence, overcoming, and even death. There are many ways to speak your way into an opportunity as well as out of one.

In the process of accomplishing any goal, one must incorporate the language of that goal. To understand goal language, one must analyze the daily habitual language that is spoken. We waste words and energy speaking nonsense but, more importantly, the words we usually choose to speak waste away our dreams. Have you truly taken the time to analyze how productive or nonproductive the language is that we use toward one another? So much of what we say to each other is plain babbling, slang, proper ways of saying nothing or educated ways of saying the wrong things. You must understand power-talking self-talk and aligning what you dream and what you mean with what you should say.

The predominant speech that we use every day, all day simply confirms the failures we experience. Think about everything that you say before you speak. Then, ask yourself if the words that you are about to speak are perpetuating the life of a goal, or the death of one?

In analyzing the words that you'll say in the future, you must revisit what's already a part of your speech repertoire. We have all adopted little sayings from people and places that we rattle off without even thinking. These very sayings are the seeds of defeat and poison that we rain on our efforts with. You may have a good vision, a great plan, but with poison speech, you get a dead harvest. It's like having fertile soil with great seeds planted, but then you saturate the planted product with product killer. You'll never have a harvest. Your entire life will be about planting promising seeds in potentially productive soil, but never getting a harvest.

The universe will never fail to be productive soil for the planting of the seeds of our dreams. We plant seeds with visions and often uproot those seeds with our speech. We then compound the problem and feel like we've been dealt a terrible hand in the poker game of life.

The moment that we speak and believe that, that's exactly what we have: a very bad hand. Our self-talk is the watering of the seeds we plant in our universal garden, so what negative things do you speak daily without carefully considering what you're saying? Here are a few things you shouldn't say that most people say out of habit:

1. This is going to be difficult for me.
2. If it wasn't for bad luck I wouldn't have any luck.
3. Knowing my luck, I won't get it, or I won't find it
4. I never win.
5. I will never get that right.
6. No one ever helps me.
7. I'm all alone.
8. I'd hate to...
9. That's a problem.
10. I'm no good at all.

11.He/she/it makes me upset.
12.I'm a procrastinator.
13.I'm lazy.
14.I really don't want to do that, but I'll see...
15.I'm really bad at names.
16.I'm really bad at apologies (or anything)

When we speak either of the statements above, we summon undesirable things in our lives. Our reply to unexpected disturbances in our lives is, "When it rains, it pours," when it is really us that turns a sprinkle into a hurricane. The shocking truth about our future is that we need to take the limits off our God and our universe as they pertain to us individually. If we train ourselves to do that and bask in the attitude of gratitude, we will then enjoy a wonderful life of amazing blessings.

What we say and believe gets in the way of what wants to come our way. We dishonor our magnificence and diminish ourselves when we say worthless things to ourselves. It's so easy to repeat negative judgments that are familiar to us about our lack of worth. We live in a time that the worst about a person is so much more believable than a person's best. A person will doubt the best that they've heard of an individual, but fully accept the negative without question or hesitation. This is representative of how a person feels about themselves. Your perception of things and how you color or judge them only identifies the relationship that you're having with yourself. The average person could hear that someone they've known their entire life did something miraculous, and it will be questioned. Let me give you an example:

We have two young men that are thirty years old and

have been the best of friends for most of their lives; or, let's can say that they've just recently become the best of friends.

One of the young men is named Rick, and the other is named Josh. Both men know that the other is not a doctor and has no doctor's knowledge. One day, Rick is at the store buying some food for dinner. Someone who knows them both stops Rick while he's shopping and says, "Rick, your boy Josh is an unbelievable guy. Someone was choking at the park a few minutes ago, and he cut the lady's throat open with a razor and stuck a straw in her neck. Blood was everywhere, but Josh was so calm. The lady started breathing through the straw. I've witnessed Josh do so many incredible things.

In most cases, Rick would be in shock and disbelief. He might go as far as to question the person that told him the story. *"Are you sure you're talking about my friend Josh?"* Now, let's use a negative example with the same two friends; except this time, this is what is said:

"Rick, you need to be careful. I just witnessed Josh stealing some money out of my coat when he thought I wasn't looking. I heard that he's been doing a lot of shady things for quite some time."

Most people who know Josh will spread the negative story of Josh before the positive one. Josh's friend, Rick, might even say out loud, *"You know, I have been noticing a few things in my apartment have come up missing lately."* That story about Josh may not even be true. Nonetheless, more people will believe the negative story and carry it to others before the good one; sometimes, the inclination to believe the negative story may be caused by jealousy or envy toward Josh because he may be a great guy. Either way, it's very easy to accept and believe the worst about others when all you believe about yourself is the worst.

In order to achieve through any challenge, you must believe that you can achieve in every challenge. Your belief system is subconsciously built or destroyed with the contribution of self-talk. Words like *sick and tired of being sick and tired*, or look bad should never be uttered.

Always speak what you want to see, and not what you feel like you are seeing at that moment. You will always manifest more of whatever you speak on the most. Saying phrases like "you make me sick" really begins the process of making you sick. Did you know that water is most receptive to speech. Scientists don't know exactly how it happens, but they know that it surely happens. Water changes when there are words of love spoken around it. When words of hate or anger are spoken, the water changed and looked poisoned or toxic under the right microscope. When a Buddhist meditated around it, the elements in it. took on yet another shape or form. Now, the applicable part to all this knowledge is the fact that ninety percent of our bodies are made up of water. Most of us really don't have a clue as to how our bodies work and how we work against ourselves, especially in the realms of speech and emotion. There is a chemical released in your body for every emotion you feel. There are chemicals for lust, hate, victimization, fear, and other emotions as well.

You can really talk yourself right out of a victory, good health, a good situation and a good life. Thus, you can talk yourself out of a bad situation and other things that surround that energy. Basically, adopting the "I Will Not Be Denied" concept means that the old concepts of speech and living need to be changed. You see, those chemicals that you have created a habit of releasing into your body have also become addictive. You become chemically attached to the same chemical. The directions that your life can go in are dependent upon certain variations of thoughts, speech, and emotion. You create the same realities, relationships, and outcomes because you have the same thoughts, feelings, and speech. You've grown accustomed to the same speech that releases a particular chemical that brings about a certain loss or failure. Many people are so conditioned to believe the way they live is the only way to live. The majority of people totally ignore the potential avenues to live different.

I've explained the importance of speech on your goals, but will you commit yourself to changing your speech? You must stop speaking illness, poison, failure, and loss. You must also stop thinking of things and think of possibilities. Life is really about a host of variations and possibilities, simply waiting for you to focus and speak on one. You must speak better things to experience better things. The brain sees more than what we realize. We must speak outside of the picture frame of what we've experienced. We only see what we believe can happen. We only believe in things that match old patterns or conditions. Yes, you read that correctly. Plainly put, you become addicted to the chemicals that are released that perpetuate your most dominant behavior and results. If you are a mediocre achiever or a person of needs and daily loses, then that's exactly what you are addicted to. The chemicals of mediocrity and loss are released by your habit of self-talk. You may be one person in your mind, until a circumstance shows you that you're someone else in your heart, but who are you out of your mouth?

Establishing success requires that you line all these energies up and position them on your goals. Thinking one thing, feeling another, and speaking something altogether different is a recipe for stagnation at best. Saying things like "this is really messed up... this crap gets on my nerves... this is bull sh__" has its own emotion attached to it from your own past

experiences. Then, those emotions have chemicals in your body that are attached to

them. Your body becomes addicted to those emotions and summons more of them. The chemicals attached to your emotional outburst of language become addictive to your body. If it's responses of disappointment and complaining that you release, then your addiction to those chemicals will summon more disappointments in your life. You may want to win, but your body may be addicted to the emotional chemical of losing.

In order to truly be an overcomer, you must not speak the language of victim. You must speak the language of victor. A victim's speech brings on victim emotions and chemicals being released into a victim's body. As sure as the blood that flows through your veins, you'll grow addicted to 'victim emotional chemicals.' As a result, your speech and emotions will summon more victim situations into your life. One must align themselves with proper language, emotion, and visualization in order to have desired results. This is one of the reasons most winners keep winning while most losers keep losing. Each person really becomes addicted to their personal formulas.

There is evidence of the power of speech in just about

every religious institution. In the Bible, it is profoundly put in the book of Mark 11 verse 23: "For verily I say unto you. That whosoever shall say unto this mountain be thou removed, and be thou cast in the sea; and shall not doubt in his heart, but shall believe that those things which he saith shall come to pass; he shall have whatsoever he saith."

When you have an undesirable situation occur in your life and you yell aloud "this situation is a pain in my side," you really believe that when you speak it. Through the releasing of the chemicals in your body, your emotions made it be just that— a pain in your side. It is essential to our future that we learn more about our inner space than our outer space. A nation that only sees what light reveals may still not see what life reveals. You cannot live right while thinking and speaking wrong. Practice ruling your speech while monitoring your thoughts and feelings. Reality accommodates intent and know-how. Tune into your inner and outer dialogue. Recognize when you have mindless chatter. Develop a heightened awareness of exactly what you are saying and how it truly impacts your life. Our misguided self-talk breaks the bridge of materialization that our creativity and ingenuity must cross.

Now, let's build a bridge for our plans, hopes, and dreams to be accelerated into completed living realities. One must develop power talk that will positively influence your entire being, those around you, and your future. Take the time to establish a new filter of thought for the words you choose to speak. Avoid the same old words of choice that have contributed to loss, disappointment, and the prevention of God blessing you. Instead of saying "I'm not good at something," say "I'm getting better."

These are just a few of the most persuasive words in the English language.

Align	Exploit	Manager
Accelerate	Evaluate	Motivate
Abolish	Focus	Overcome
Capture	Foresee	Persuade
Change	Finalize	Plan
Comprehend	Find	Prepare
Confront	Grasp	Profit
Connect	Gain	Refresh
Conquer	Generate	Replace
Convert	Gather	Retain
Create	Implement	Respond
Deliver	Improve	Shatter
Design	Increase	Succeed
Diagnose	Innovate	Supplement
Discover	Lead	Transfer
Eliminate	Learn	Transform
Ensure	Master	Understand
		Unleash

We are born powerful and persuasive, but choose to use words and phrases that diminish and reduce our power. There are hundreds of powerful and persuasive words, and just as many ways to use them. I just chose to include a few in this chapter to set you down the path. However, it is you that must walk the path. Some of the greatest speeches ever written all had one thing in common. They were riddled with most of the same persuasive words but used differently. I am not saying one particular word has this super magic to build or destroy your life; I am saying that because of the emotions we have attached to words, we must raise our awareness of the words we use.

Here are some much better choices of words to use than the ones I used earlier in this chapter. Think of them as examples of power speaking:

1. I am looking forward to the challenging opportunities.
2. I create my opportunities with hard work and faith.
3. No matter how it appears, it will work out for my benefit.
4. I will find it if it's there to find.
5. I will benefit from the experience.
6. I am getting better at doing this.
7. I'm growing at my relationship skills.
8. I'm strong enough to handle this.
9. I would like to...
10. I'll learn a lot from this opportunity.

11. I'm delighted to do this.
12. I am in control of how I feel.
13. I'm getting better at not putting things off.
14. I choose to not put things off anymore.
15. No! I won't do it because I don't feel comfortable.
16. I'm getting better at names.
17. When I'm wrong, I must apologize.

Please flip back to the beginning of this chapter and reflect on the sixteen things that you shouldn't say. Affirmations are a must in order to send the right energy and chemicals flowing through you and around you.

A. I accept the trials and hardships that have helped shape me. They have helped me to be an overcomer. Nothing is greater than the power in me from the God I serve.

B. I think the very best of myself at all times. I have aligned my consciousness with that of the supreme consciousness and because of that, I am full of grace, confidence, wealth, health, and happiness. I am not a victim. I am victorious over all that comes against me because nothing is greater than the flow of life that runs through me.

C. I am transformed and maximized by that which has destroyed most, for I am the instrument of hope and growth when others have very little. I learn from C. experiences, but I am not imprisoned by them. I was born free to see no limits C. above, below, or next to me. Thus, I am guaranteed by those truths that there are none inside of me.

D. I don't see problems! I see solutions and opportunities. I have aligned all my energies with the right formulas of the universe. I am in harmony with all, and that means that all is at my access. I am developed and deployed in the greatest favors of God. I can't be denied.

E. I measure how great my life is, not how great my problems are! I persuade opposition to get in the correct position. I lead others with my silence and heavenly guidance. I do not doubt or boast with my mouth. I am immortalized and maximized when I allow truth to immobilize and finalize. I side-step critics and therefore, confusion is simplified. Misunderstandings are always clarified because my spiritual inheritance is to confront, connect, and conquer after I identify.

F. I am open to and aware of my higher power. I am no longer shackled by the limited, everyday self. My higher self gives me love and protection. I discover new regions in myself every moment of every day. I am fortunate to know that I am connected to the source of all the answers, which flows freely to me when I sit calmly. I am ensured that the design of my life is boundless and cannot be destroyed by the whims of humanity. I shatter all obstacles in my way. Through my God, I master my life.

G. I gain favor through service, but no task makes me nervous. I foresee trouble, and the universe exploits its governor. I assess risk, but I don't fear danger. I am God's child and have a grasp of his courage. I eliminate emotional addictions that don't increase my value to the world. I win because I was born to. I inspire because I was led to. I conquer in each moment because I was prepared to. I convert all ailments into a healthy flow of energy, build bridges of truth, and break chains of lies. I uplift the discouraged and adopt the abandoned. I apply knowledge and gather sheep. I respect and treat people fairly because I know I must sow what I seek to reap.

These are just simple phrases that you may put together to nourish and feed your soul.

I would like to close out this chapter with more vital information. This great nation of people that we have is growing into a bunch of runners and pouters. Both in and out of prison, everyone seems to shut down and shut off people close to them when they are going through adversity. That is the very worst thing that you could do. Most people are tired of people lying to them, putting them off, and not keeping their word.

FEAR

I am very convinced that every person on Earth is afraid of something. Most of the fears that people have are inherited, culturally initiated, or simply derived from unfavorable circumstances. I like to break fear down as fabricated emotion altering reality. It is the anticipation of particular events that we attach the most disturbing emotions to. In order to be successful or advance on any level, you must always have the courage to face your fears. Respect an element, but don't fear It. Not facing your fears cripples your ability to accomplish and blocks the fluid nature of your energy. Others fear being successful. They fear being seen and examined on a large scale; being the heart of some compliments from people, yet severely ridiculed by others.

Fear of success, failure, death, embarrassment, and so many other things can be

debilitating. I encourage you to attack your fears aggressively, but calmly. Every time you do, you will feel yourself getting stronger and stronger. When a lot of the fears in your life go unchallenged, your so-called successes are actually leftover debris of the real magnitude of what your successes could be.

Having respect for a situation means you will attempt with all your might to refrain from violating other persons; it means you will be considerate of the presence of others and what they represent. Nonetheless, if purpose arises, you will handle others with care.

When I was incarcerated, I remember telling myself that I was going to attack as many of my fears as possible. One was a childhood fear of needles. In 2007, I made up my mind to attack and face that fear. I signed up for every blood, TB, and HIV test and as much dental work as I could. I had nine fillings put in my mouth, and I was stuck in my arms at least ten times. I was liberated from that experience and became empowered by the victory. Now, keep in mind that it takes much more than confronting the fear over and over to free. yourself of it. You must change your mindset of the fear before and during the experience of overcoming it.

In the process of defeating my fear of needles, the first thing I did was work on my anticipation of the pain before the needle came. Through self-talk and self-realization, I trained myself to believe there was nothing to concern myself with before and after insertion. There was nothing to concern myself with because it was over. I reinforced that mindset with the acknowledgement of the fact that I was not a fleshy being, but instead, a spiritual being having a human or fleshly experience. The mere focus on these words and the meaning behind them raises you above conditions of the flesh.

What everyone must realize is that whatever you fear, you draw to yourself. Therefore, it does you no good to be deathly afraid of anything because you're almost guaranteeing yourself to come face to face with it. Confronting it on your own terms is empowering for you. It suggests to you a feeling of being able to overcome. Building the confidence that you are an overcomer also builds faith that you can achieve. There is no way to truly advance in life without facing your fears. It's the prerequisite of change. Facing your fears is the release of counterproductive energy while summoning the empowering energy. The false perceptions of consequences and the ills that they bring has slowed people down for centuries. There are fears that I believe are collective consciousness fears; simply put, group fears.

A lot of these fears are passed down emotionally from loved ones and environmental influences. I've witnessed thousands of men not pursue what is due to them in prison because out of fear of losing prison privileges, or fear of upsetting an officer to the point where the officer lies and gets the inmate in trouble. I mean, an inmate who is sick and in need of medical treatment will not pursue it for fear of upsetting a lazy officer. For me, I always felt like as long as I was in prison there is no such thing as a real privilege. Everything in prison was simply implemented to calm some of the roaring thoughts that result from being held against your will. Henceforth, an inmate doesn't say or do anything about the violations against him or her, all in an effort to hold on to superficial privileges that keep them numb to what their situation really is.

Like I mentioned in my book *Nothing to Waste in the Wasteland*, you can't be afraid of discomfort. Only when you feel uncomfortable do you create and innovate. One must first welcome an internal revolution in order to have an evolution. I've seen men die in prison from having a heart attack. While it may have been preventable, they were afraid to go to the doctor at the first sign of chest pains a few days prior to their death. They were afraid of the diagnosis, or of something dealing with the medical field environment.

I've also seen a couple of prisoners die who went to

the prison nurse due to chest pains, but allowed the nurse to dismiss the pains as gas or indigestion. Later that week or the next, they died of heart failure. They were too afraid to be more aggressive, dramatic, and demanding about going to a real doctor or hospital to be checked thoroughly.

In most prisons, you have to be really aggressive or dramatic in order to have a chance of getting proper medical treatment. Most prisoners that need it don't get it, and some die as a result. I mean, their fears really killed them or caused them greater damage.

Fears are what some people rely on in order to control other people. Fear is a mass population controller on so many fronts. Plenty of opportunities are missed due to people being trapped in fear. Being a risk taker is the one element that I will not eradicate from my personal arsenal. Many people read and speak of faith, but do not walk in it. I've come to the consciousness that faith is developed over time. It's built through survival of struggles throughout your personal path.

Faith is not seeing a thing or a condition present, yet knowing it is there or on its way. Faith is God's promise of deliverance and you moving in the spirit as though it has already arrived. To walk in faith is to be bold and brave when you need to be. Sometimes, the "I'll do it next time," mentality doesn't work. Often times, there is no *next time*. There is only *this*

time. Everything is the build-up for what's about to appear in your life. When you miss it, it's sometimes gone forever. I can remember a very valuable lesson about truth that I learned during my summer vacation to Detroit when I was barely sixteen years of age.

I went to Northland Roller Rink on Eight Mile Road, as I usually did every Saturday during the summer. On this particular Saturday, I noticed a very beautiful young lady in the skating rink that I had never seen before. She was so beautiful to me that I actually felt my heart skip a beat as my stomach dropped. After noticing her several times as I walked to get my skates and get situated, I sort of lost track of her. I enjoyed sitting on the bench and just watching others skate to the music. That's what I decided to do on that particular day.

Upon sitting on the side, I finally noticed the stunningly beautiful young lady come pearling by on her skates. On top of her being gorgeous, she could also skate with the best of them in the building. To my surprise, though, when she came rolling past me, she looked at me and gave me a smile. Of course, in shock at what I just noticed, I looked around myself twice to see if that smile was really for me. The next time she came flying by, I looked into her eyes carefully, and she gazed even harder the second time. With each lap she made around the rink, our communication got bolder. At one point, she waved at me and I waved back. At that point, it felt like every other person in that entire skating rink disappeared in our minds. We watched each other like hawks. One time, I purposely got up and went to buy some popcorn, just to see if she would miss me. Sure enough, when she came around to where I previously sat, I noticed her almost fall on her skates while attempting to scan the building for me.

A slow song came on, and I will never forget it. It was *Fire and Desire* by Rick James and Tina Marie. By the time I got back to my seat, the beautiful young lady was skating backward, wrapped up in some young man's arms. Of course, I didn't like it, even though she still stared at me as she passed by. The second time she passed me in his arms, I hunched my shoulders and opened up the palms of my hands, basically making the gesture to ask "What's up with that?" I knew that I was pushing it with that, but I went for it anyway. It worked! She gave me a quiet head nod and frowned as if to say, "No, I'm just skating with him."

When she made that third lap, she had dislodged herself from the young guy and was no longer slow skating with him. I knew then that she really liked me. She had given me every hint, signal, and sign in the book. All signs had shown me to go up and introduce myself, or at least summon .her to come over to where I was. Instead, I punked out! I was too scared to say anything to her. We flirted with each other with our eyes for almost four hours.

When it was time to leave the skating rink, she picked a bench right by the exit door. I was on the opposite side of the building at the time but nonetheless, she kept glancing up as she pretended to pack her things; she was really watching me make my way around to her side. As I got closer to her and to the exit, I heard a couple of other young girls yelling at her to hurry up.

As I got closer to her, I got even more nervous and frightened. She glanced up at me as I walked my scared self right passed her and out the exit. I didn't say goodbye or wave or anything. I told myself that I would build up more courage the following week and would surely talk to her then. I was totally convinced that she would be returning the following Saturday.

It has been roughly twenty-eight years since that day, and I've never seen that young lady again. I went back to that skating rink every Saturday after that special day, and she wasn't there. This went on for every Spring Break, Christmas break, and summer vacation for the next two years after that day. Even to this day, I think about that day. It's bigger than the young lady. It's about the missed opportunity to interact with another being that God has breathed life into. Who was she? What may I have learned from her? What may I have shared with her?

I don't live in regret, but she helped to change how I see fear. I told myself that I will not ever be frozen in fear like that again. I have a good friend who always says, I can take no for an answer, but I won't take no answer." Sometimes, you have to experience something in order to truly comprehend that. Throughout these years, I've adopted the next level to the *I won't take NO For an answer* thing. Mine is *I Will Not Be Denied.* In the Bible, in Matthew, it is stated as, "For God never' gave you a spirit of fear but of love, power and of sound mind."

Like I always say to people, if you live in fear and what's been shown to you, then where do your instincts and intuitions fit in? I move off my spirit and instincts now. I realize that most people are controlled by their fears. Others prepare for their big moment in life and allow fear to move it right on past them. Every decision that I need to make has signs to help me make it. I just need to always move beyond fear. Move toward what you fear, and the fear will disappear. Fear binds you. Fear can become a habit for some. They actually live in fear of everything. A few of the greatest enemies of achievement are fear, doubt, and second-guessing.

This journey is about experiences and mastering the self. You are not your beliefs, habits or attitudes. You were taught these things. The majority of society only believes in what they see. If you're in a situation of lack and restriction and only put credence in what exists, then how can you even obtain what you dream or hope for?

Our minds are so subject to the dominating influences in our environments. We must take back control of our minds and move in conjunction with a spirit of cooperation with the natural flow of things. Fear, doubt, resentment, envy, and jealousy are not a natural part of the universal flow within. Instead, those are all blockages. When faced with a crossroad, always take the road that scares you the most, but it is lined up with righteousness. I must live in the "now" moment. I refuse to let fear scare me out of this moment into the next, where fear shall be waiting once more, always seeking to procrastinate me. No, no, no, no!

I see who fear is, and I attack him ferociously. I know the handicaps that he brings and know that he lives in me, but only when I feed him. Starve fear and feed instincts but develop faith in that process. With each accomplishment, no matter how small, grow stronger. Don't let people around you transfer their fears into you. You already inherited your own that you must fight through. Then, you truly will know, face-to-face, the power of fearless living.

When you apply the tools mentioned in this book, you

shall be granted a higher walk of consciousness.

The truth is all around you. You don't need to have it shown to you. Simply open your mind's eye and see what you feel and when you feel it. Gain control of your mind's fears and you will begin to gain back your future.

EXPECT THE MAGIC

I once read somewhere that if you combined all the wisdom from the greatest minds that ever walked this earth, it would still only be a drop of water in the sea of untapped wisdom. Yet, know that sea of untapped wisdom is accessible to each and every one of us. When you believe, speak, talk, and walk in that truth, magic happens. That sea is where magic flows.

Magic is the result of a conscious effort of alignment with what appears to be the mysteries of the universe. When you move in agreement with all that has been written in this book, you must too expect the magic. The word "magic" in most dictionaries is defined as "the supposed art of influencing the course of events supernaturally." Another of its definitions is "producing surprising results." Every problem that has ever confronted every human at any time has always been insulated with magic. It has always been a person's alignment with the elements of magic, and then the ignition of expectancy. What I call magic has been called so many other things by so many people. I once read an article in *Time Magazine* about something called "The God Gene." Educators were mentioning it as well.

I've read up on material dealing with quantum physics and metaphysics. All scientists and doctors, in some way, state that there are some things they just cannot explain; some kind of point in any situation where the body pulls off miraculous results. One of the most important keys in your formula of success should be "what do you expect to happen?" After you have visualized, verbalized, and internalized it, what are you expecting to happen from all you have done?

I have learned, through every breath I take and every moment I live in, to expect magic to happen. I anticipate the magic of going directly to the needle in the haystack. Everything that happens in life is strictly for direction, and you must realize that you shall see what you expect to see. I expect magic in all my situations, so much so that I sometimes don't get a chance to expect the magic before magic happens. I'm a supernatural being from a supernatural source, so why wouldn't I expect supernatural things to happen to me? Magic!

One day, while I was in the Federal Prison Camp Atlanta, I was on my way to lunch. I worked on the landscape detail. On this particular day, I was coming down a hill and noticed what I believed to be a large blue garbage can lid lying in the middle of the grass. My landscape foreman, Mr. Wayne Tuck (God rest his soul), once told me that a landscaper should never walk past something misplaced and leave it as such.

Taking his training to heart, I bent down to pick up the large lid that I believed had obviously blown off some large container. Lid in hand, I took another step in the direction of going down the hill toward the chow hall. Suddenly, the earth fell beneath the stepping foot as I attempted to land it. Before I could mentally process what was happening to my body, I was in a death drop, going down a fifteen-foot manhole. Miraculously, while dropping, my rib cage smashed into the concrete and steel mouth of the hole. The impact bounced my body like a rag doll, and my armpit lodged on the side of the manhole.

Here I was, dangling with one arm holding me from dropping. Some kind of way, I was able to grab on with the second arm and pull myself all the way out. I then realized that I was struggling to breathe. Only then did the piercing pain to my ribs become apparent. One of the other prisoners ran up to assist me, but when he got close, he locked in on the possibly gruesome possible death drop. "Oh my God!" he yelled out, stuck looking down the manhole. He actually went into shock staring into the mouth of death for me.

It took a second, third, and fourth fellow prisoner to come before I really received assistance. Of course, the officer ran to my aid as soon as he was notified. I couldn't breathe, and my ribs were causing me unbearable pain. I was rushed to the doctor by the officer to be x-rayed and examined. What I didn't' t realize was that many prisoners and staff witnessed me disappear into the earth. To everyone's surprise, I didn't have one broken rib. A large bruise where the break could've been was the only damage.

Laughing, coughing, and talking caused me great discomfort for several months after the incident. The day after I was released from the doctor, I had someone help me walk back up to the manhole. I wanted to look at the place that could've taken my life. I was stunned at the huge mouth and the depth of the hole. Correctional officers were all placing blame on each other regarding why the hole was uncovered. My foreman, Mr. Tuck, was quick to claim the oversight. It wasn't his fault, though, but he was full of integrity like that. Other onlookers were all mumbling the words "lawsuit" and "suing." I was full of gratitude to God. There was absolutely no other way I could've survived that ordeal with just badly bruised ribs. Let me try to make you see this situation clearly.

Picture the fact that I was already walking down a grass-covered hill, which means my body was positioned forward and I stepped with my right foot into a very wide-mouthed manhole. At the very least, a broken jaw, snapped neck, or concussion from crashing my head into the edge would have been expected injuries. Keep in mind that would have been me sustaining those injuries by catching myself. I won't go into actually dropping fifteen feet and crashing up against concrete and a steel ladder all the way down to the bottom.

About two nights after my incident, I was watching the news and they reported that a woman died dropping into a ten-foot manhole. The reporter said that she sustained injuries to her face and broke her neck during the drop. The reporter went on to state that had been the second manhole incident that year. The person who previously fell in a manhole survived but was permanently paralyzed. My body was positioned forward and I stepped forward, but the left side of my rib cage and armpit crashed into the side of the mouth of the manhole, just long enough to hang on with an elbow to grab on with the other arm. The doctor who examined me that day asked me if I worked out. After I told her that I had been working out for years, she attributed my strength to pull myself out to that. I disagreed. Most of my friends who knew that I had been doing pull-ups for over ten years also agreed with her. My pull-up strength would have done me absolutely no good if I hit my chin or face on the edge of that manhole going down or crashed my head back and forth between those concrete walls while headed to the bottom. I'm thankful to God for surviving that and I have one word to describe it: magic!

Each magical testimony is birthed from another magical story.

I was charged in federal court with the 848 CCE Statue, which is nicknamed the infamous kingpin charge. In the Federal Bureau of Prisons, anyone charged as a drug kingpin is forbidden from ever going to a federal prison camp. A federal prison camp is a minimum-security prison, usually with no fence around it, and possible daily interaction with the community. For someone charged with a kingpin charge, it takes all kinds of recommendations and security waivers to get that individual to a camp. The recommendations would have to come from high-ranking bureau officers, like unit managers, assistant wardens, and wardens. The waiver would need to come from the regional director who is over the warden.

Well, to even get to the Atlanta camp where I had the near-death experience, it took magic. I had instructed five and six different classes a week while also being a student in three others before I was granted federal camp status. I was life coaching and teaching self-development material to hundreds of prisoners a week. Correctional officers would even sit in on some of my groups. Several times, I noticed staff being moved to tears just listening to lectures in my group. One of my mentor groups at the Elkton, Ohio federal prison facility had at least seventy-five attendants. There was at least a year-long waiting list to get into my class. It was called "Highly Success Living." Staff and inmates always mentioned that I caused magic to happen on that compound.

In 2009, a very courageous and bold professional unit manager came to my unit in the Elkton facility. I was always told by other prison staff that I would have to do all my prison time at that facility. When Mr. J. Streeval came to Elkton and became my unit manager, that view changed. He said because of all my unbelievable achievements in prison, he was going to fight for me to be sent to a prison camp. He did that and made even more magic happen.

In October of 2009, my kingpin restriction was waived by the regional director to allow me to go to a camp. I chose to go to the Atlanta, Georgia Prison Camp. More magic happened. I was given money and released out of the Ohio facility to take myself to the camp in Atlanta. It's called a prison furlough. I was given a 27- hour furlough to take myself to the Atlanta, Georgia prison camp. The terms of my furlough were to catch a Greyhound bus to Atlanta, Georgia and purchase a taxi cab to the facility. Many people marveled at me being able to go to a camp and receiving a furlough, especially since I went to trial on my case and never assisted the government in incarcerating other alleged criminals. The magical process of getting to the camp happened before the manhole magic.

Every day I breathe, I line myself up, rebalance, and expect magic. There are so many splendid marvels in this universe, and so many miracles waiting to be called upon. There are just as many miracles in the universe to be let loose as there are atoms to be used in matter. Success always lies half asleep in the same bed with failure. You choose your bed mate, and their magnitude of awakening is based upon your efforts in alignment and the expectations of what they produce. When you expect magic, you convert mediocre events into magnificence. Poisons will turn into productions, and suppressions into successes. Life will always turn out to be what you work for and expected it to be for yourself. People don't affect reality at great lengths because they don't expect to.

We are the greatest miracle in the world, so in everything I do, I expect magic and miracles. When you've done the work, there is only one thing left to do. That is: don't blink because you might miss the miracle." That has been my personal motto since the first day of my incarceration.

Expect the Magic!

DEFIANCE TO THE DELIVERANCE

Mental toughness is to endure daily tests of beliefs, confidence, and determination. You may be beat in the face with rejection day after day. Resilience is always your best friend when there's a place you're trying to reach. Being fierce during challenging times is a mindset you develop from coming through challenging times. You develop an intrinsic formula that acts as an automatic self-realignment with the natural solution when you push through to the end. Just keep enduring, creating emotions of already overcoming what is currently challenging you. You must walk in the deliberate action of all the tools presented in this book, only leaving the massively magical medicine of expectations.

Everything can be a curse and a blessing. You must be defiant when your blessings take on the perspective of a curse; timing and perspective can alter which side of the pendulum that energy rests on. Someone that has been a blessing to you at certain points in your process of life can transform into a burden at the wrong time. It's the wrong time because all your focus and resources must be gathered and directed toward the desired goal. Be defiant to the interruption and distraction. Don't feed into the sense of obligation.

Be steadfast in all energies that lead to your manifested dreams. Be defiant until the deliverance. When I say defiant, I mean defying everything that your spirit doesn't direct you to incorporate. One must be defiant to discouragement, a false sense of pride, laziness, overindulging pleasures, counterproductive language, counterproductive friends and family, too much sleep, impatience, too much eating, too much eating of the wrong foods, too much watchfulness, too much talking, and definitely too much listening to the wrong things. Walk away!

If you don't appear to be the daily odd ball when you're pursuing something, then you're nowhere near being on the right track. Defiance is usually distance from what our surroundings say is normalcy. In the dawn of the accomplishment, you will most definitely have invaders coming to destroy the objective. These invaders may range from personal relationships and bad habits to unexpected financial pressures and health issues for you or a loved one. As cold as this may sound, at the end of the day, these things are invaders. If you're looking for excuses to not complete the mission, then excuses are available. If you feel like no excuse is good enough to stop you, then no excuse is powerful enough. You won't recognize anything but your dream being manifested. All that I've enclosed in this book amounts to a system of production. It produces whatever you choose to produce. The defiance is the self-contained security system in that protects the production of the heart's desires. Let's compare this system to the system in the body, the system that is naturally defiant toward any foreign elements.

Have you ever watched how defiant your immune system is when colds, flus, or certain invaders penetrate to your system? Your immune system attacks the invaders with a fierce defiance. It continues to be defiant until the deliverance, until the body is totally rescued from the infestation. The lesson to be learned from the immune system is a much-needed one. Have you ever witnessed how white blood cells in your body attack invaders in the system? It doesn't matter if it's one invader or tons of them. Your system attacks them with the same ferocious tenacity. Under the microscope, it looks like a hundred elements devouring one, a great example of "Defiance to the Deliverance."

Without defiance, you will not be able to withstand the invaders of your system that materialize your dreams. Being defiant to the deliverance is a protective mentality. You are saying that you are grateful for being brought to the brink of success, and nothing will send you backward. Nothing will stall God's promise of deliverance. The immune system that you're born with is simply a testimony of protective defiance. It's the nature of parasites to draw to the light. You are the light and the more you are aligned, the greater you shine. Equally so, the more parasites and bugs appear in your life.

Be defiant to continue to shine despite interruptions and viruses of all kinds. This is not a complicated issue at all. Actually, all you have to do is keep the interferences if your life from interfering with the natural flow of your deliverance. Be defiant of counterproductive behavior from others or self. Dispute irrational thinking that brings about self-sabotage. If you can break these words down in your spirit and understand how they apply to your personal goals, you are ready to align yourself with all of them simultaneously.

Direction

Discipline

Deliverance

Dedication

Defiance

I know enough to know that I know very little
about what I could know, but what I do know
appears to be so much to everyone because they
don't know what they should know. What they
could know is proliferated, then lost in too much
chatter about what they don't know, but think
they do know. First, you have to acquire the need
to know by dropping the arrogance in what you
seem to know because there is a deeper theme to
know. There was a leader's dream to show.
What's now easy for you to read to know, others
had to sneak or bleed to know.

Now, knowledge is like oxygen. It's everywhere and
we take it for granted. Everyone claims that we're born
equal, but we're not equal now. The knowledge is
slanted. Contrary to what you were told, nothing will be
handed nothing to hold when you're mentally stranded.

PURPOSE

An intellectual friend of mine inspired a much deeper explanation of this topic. One day, I was strolling along on the Atlanta prison compound and he stopped me and said, "How is your book coming along, and what chapter are you on now?" I replied, "I'm almost done with it. I have a couple chapters or topics left. Right now, I'm about to write on the topic of purpose."

He then looked at me with a face full of confusion and said, "If you're writing a self-help book of sorts, why would you address purpose at the end of the book? Wouldn't it make more sense to place the chapter on purpose in the beginning of the book? Surely, people need to know their purpose before they do anything else..."

That brief exchange of words I had with that very intelligent-sound friend, inspired me to expound on this topic in depth. Throughout life's journey, many people in pursuit of more internal fulfillment from life will speak of purpose. Most will simply request and question aloud, saying, "I want to know my purpose. I don't know my purpose..." How do you know what your purpose is? This question and those comments have plagued millions of people for generations and generations. I will shed a little light on this topic in the hope that you connect with your higher consciousness."

First of all, I placed the chapter of purpose toward the back of this book because that's usually when you figure things out— at the end of a situation. We live, but desire to live a life of aim and purpose. Nonetheless, purpose is not what you should do; it lies within what you already are doing. It is the intent of your self-created, deliberate destiny. We come from a multipurpose God who strategically arranges events of our choosing.

Purpose is about consciousness creating motion in space; our consciousness creating realities that inspire us to move in time and space to create and dictate agendas. Simply put, you must have meaning in your motion. One day while getting my hair cut in prison, my barber asked, "Brother, I struggle with knowing my purpose. I feel I have all the tools. Can you help me identify my purpose? It's like I have the nails, hammer, saw, screwdriver, and the pliers. I just don't know what to do with them."

I have found that the old adage applies to his question: "The best place to hide something is in plain sight." Thus, it is with your purpose. Each tool that you may possess is deliberately created for its particular purpose. The key to life is to recognize and develop your tools and keep the toolbox ready. When the tools are present, the purpose for them will always appear.

Each collision and completion with tools and purpose, brings fulfillment of micro-purpose in the big scheme of the larger purpose. So many people stress themselves out on finding their purpose, not realizing that purpose brought them here to this point in time, this very moment in which you are reading and enjoying this book. As I mentioned previously in this chapter, your purpose is in what you are doing, not in what you think you should be doing. The moment you think too much, you've drifted out of purpose and into programming. People will actually stop what they're doing to think and stress about doing something else.

Purpose is to create something out of nothing, to create activity of meaning where there may be none, and to contribute to the collaborating activities of directed energies. Anything left to itself will deteriorate. When you still have problems uncovering your self-hidden purpose, just assist others with theirs and yours will come. Service to others is the great magical element that brings all purposes forward. Success and fulfillment hide their pretty faces in the reflection of service. This wonderful universe of ours will never reveal to you your purpose because it simply accommodates your tools. It responds to your inherent commands. There isn't a life form not responsible for its resulting energies. The purpose of anyone is not defined by the condition or situation in which he or she stands, but in the direction that they are moving in.

So much of what we do is shaped by those closest to us. Our surroundings sometimes shade who we really are and replace that with who others might be, but that is our fault. We are designed with our own individual reason for breathing. That particular trade, skill, or direction encompasses that exact purpose: why our life is so important. Anyone that believes they are here to just exist begins the process to cease to exist. There's a war between who the world sees we are and who we really are.

In the fumes and ashes of exchange, lie the identity chain. Maximize all energies in your endeavors, and purpose will suddenly join you and transform your thoughts. Let's look at a deeper "what if."

What if I told you the purpose of your life was to be doing exactly what you are doing right now? What would you say, and how would you feel? What if before you were born, you chose to go through everything that you've gone through in your life thus far? Would you be at peace then? Sometimes, the questions transform into answers when we change the position of perspective.

THE PRICE OF FAME

If you're willing to pay a price high enough, you can do anything. However, no one tells you that when you do the "anything," there may be a continuous tax. Everything comes with an enclosed tax. It's enclosed because you won't really know the tax until you're being taxed. It's the tax of fame that can be so high that you'll wish you could return fame back to the store of the universe, all in exchange for your money (life) back. You see, the price of fame can cost you friends, family, your peace of mind, and even your life.

Before I get into just how that happens, let's establish what fame is. The American Heritage College Dictionary defines fame as "great renown." It also defines it as, "public estimation; reputation," meaning you don't have to be some big Hollywood movie star to have fame or a reputation for doing something. For example, there may be a particular person in your family who is known for cooking great meals. That individual has what I call "soft fame." Everyone and anyone who knows that person usually calls that person to prepare dishes on special occasions.

Just for the sake of me making my point, let's say that person is your grandmother (in most families, they've been the best cooks). Now, let's examine what your grandmother will have to deal with. First off, most of the family, friends, and her church will probably be inconsiderate of her personal time. They want what they want. Everyone will turn to her to cook for any and every occasion. Some people will make up an occasion to get her to cook. Grandmother will deal with jealousy from the wives of some men, who despise the grandmother because their husbands would rather eat her cooking.

People who go to grandmother will never think about the vast amount of seasoning and vegetables that she uses up. No one will replace the seasoning or care about the clean-up after the process of preparing the meals. People will put on a superficial showing by asking her, "how are you doing" but their energies are saying they're more concerned about their dishes being prepared. She will deal with pressure, stress, financial demands, inconsiderate behavior, and betrayal; she becomes a target. People will suddenly compete with her, slander some of her meals, and others will drain her dry. A very small percentage will truly appreciate what she does and make a genuine effort to show her immense gratitude. All of this being said, grandmother has no reason to complain because this is the price of fame.

Some of the readers may feel that everyone deals with those depleting issues, even the ones who are not famous; however, not to the same degree as the individuals who are standouts in a particular area. An individual with fame must develop skills to cope with fame. All the elements of fame have destroyed countless lives. Many famous entertainers have wished they could go backward and not have the level of fame they experienced. The lifestyle has promoted drug abuse on all levels. Many famous people have to take depressants to go to sleep at night and stimulant drugs to get going in the morning when they wake up. A question to ask yourself is, "When you acquire what it is you have worked for, are you ready for its tax?" Will the obtaining of your dreams cost you your inner peace and all the divine gifts of life?

Once you get the internal questions of fame, then you must journey to external questions, such as "Do you really know how to live with fame? Do you know how to protect yourself, your children, family, friends, possessions, and your career?"

All the illusions of fame and success have inspired many men to trade in the trusted, reliable, and proven wife for the unproven, superficially, beautified shadow of one. I know a nation of women who just read that and are encouraging me to say more. Well, guess what? Women, you do it too. Without saying names, there are so many women who were in good relationships before their big break and deliberately sabotaged that relationship. They broke up with the good guy that they grew up dating to date a guy in the industry who had a thousand women on his rough day— just for the sake of dating a household name. It may work out for some, but most end up wishing they had a good, honest mate outside of the fame circuit.

When your fame, money, and popularity go up, you must stay grounded. As you've read in this chapter so far, fame can destroy many aspects of your life. I hope you are strapped in good to this book, because I'm just getting started in this chapter. Many people have gone into deep depression due to not being able to adjust to the fame game. Some have even committed suicide under the pressures of fame. People on Wall Street have lost money and status in a day and chosen to take their own lives over facing their loved ones. People who once lived in affluent communities and lost their fortune have run away from their responsibilities. I mean, they actually kissed the wife and kids on the way to work but chose never to go home again when they got off work.

It doesn't have to be the loss after once having fame that inspires destructive choices. You can be right in the middle phase of super fame and you may still destroy yourself. These messages go all the way back in time. We may use King Solomon in the Bible for a good example. He had the greatest wisdom in the land and the lifestyle to go with it. He had over a thousand women, and he ultimately fell out of harmony with his spiritual alignment. You may have always heard the quote, "Be careful what you ask for because you just might get it."

It takes a certain kind of life coach to guide a person on how to live with instant fame. The best person to do that is not a famous person, nor is it a therapist of any sort. It's a person who has come from nothing, been cast into instant fame themselves, and yet managed to keep the pieces of their life together. Most people desire a lifestyle that they absolutely couldn't handle if they achieved it.

When you accelerate from one dimension of life through several others, to a more enriched illusionary aspect of life without the mental evolutionary process to go with it, then you are destined for many disasters. Your safety net must be your support team. You must surround yourself with genuine people who will hold you accountable for your decisions, individuals who are not scared to tell you that you are making bad, irresponsible choices if you are doing so.

I'm not going to say what most people say. Most people say that nothing is greater than your family, that your family will be there for you no matter what. That is not necessarily true. Sometimes, your family will jump ship faster than your friends will. Therefore, I will say to you that family is as family does. Yes, blood is thicker than water, but the spirit is thicker than it all. Often, it may be your birth family that places the most insensitive burdens on you. Other times, your family may be your truest group. I'm just saying, don't use your genes to distinguish who will be good for you. Let your higher power guide you. Evaluate that intuitively. This is the part of the chapter where I go into your emotions with this message. You won't truly grasp this message until you attach your emotions to it.

Anytime there is a disparity between what you

possess and what the next person possesses, you must be prepared for them to possibly be possessed with you. That possession may be expressed in an abundance of ways. Your job is not to concern yourself with their insecurities with you, but to guard yourself (and your surroundings) from the harmful expressions of their insecurities. You must realize that you can't keep what you can't protect. It's not about being paranoid or fearful. It's about making it difficult to harm you or your loved ones.

The hardest enemy to protect yourself from is the one that you don't even know exists.

Fame, success, lifestyle advantages, and even intelligence may ignite high levels of evil and treachery in the least likely people. When many people compliment you about anything in particular, that is your warning sign that you are standing out. Don't fear it, though. Embrace it, but move accordingly.

Too many people in this country underachieve because of the fear of being a target, or not being accepted in the land of mediocrity. We are here to maximize our potentials, evolve, and let our light of life shine bright. I'm just letting you know that each dimension of any lifestyle comes with its own demands. In order to survive. Learn how to survive and thrive in that dimension or suffer the consequences, which might be a price that is so costly that you may lose your wits trying to pay it.

It's a cold reality of what comes with being famous in any field on every level. What you are illustrating is those supreme beings or supernatural traits that remind others of their inadequacies. Therefore, they either want to see you fail, or they desire to take what you have. For others, they are moved and inspired by what you show them in your walk of life. That's the positive aspect that you allow to fuel your actions. Nonetheless, you must protect yourself because there is always a price for fame. If you simply analyze my life, I paid a price for always being a standout. Early in this book, I wrote about how I was famous for having a big head. I suffered ridicule by friends, family, and onlookers. The ridicule is one of the prices I paid. It was the same with the speech impediment. Fame doesn't have to come from something you desire to be famous for. You can be famous for having bad breath. There will definitely be a price to pay for that kind of fame. People will offer you peppermints, even stepping back when you speak, and do whatever possible to create physical separation between the two of you. All jokes aside, though, I hope you get the point.

I've realized how valuable the lessons are that I've learned while selling drugs, and how they can protect anyone in ordinary everyday life. While selling drugs, you are reminded every day you wake up that you are a target; if not just for the fact that you are selling drugs, then by the value of my material possessions. The best lessons are the hard lessons that truly capture your attention and penetrate your comfort. Let me bring you into those cemented lessons about how I learned how to live with fame.

The lessons that I've learned the hard way are why I decided to create a career counseling individuals that have come into instant fame or substantial income. Your behavior, the way you treat people, and your habits can nullify whatever blessings of money or fame that you have acquired.

Warning: this next material may be graphic or cause offense to some readers. This a disclaimer to release myself of any responsibility for any emotions or feelings for this next material. It is only written to aid and assist you in living a healthier and safer life.

Do you have an infant that is maybe a few weeks old or know a relative who has an infant that is young? Imagine you and your spouse come home from a nice evening out. Your infant is in the car seat behind you. You and your spouse can't go a whole block in the car without glancing back at your precious, new innocent baby. That dazzling smile on your child's face is just so irresistible to look at. Well, you, your mate, and your infant pull up in front of your cozy home that you feel safe in. As soon as you get out of the car, you are surprised and greeted by a masked man with a gun. You turn to look at your significant other, and they're greeted with the same fate by another gunman on the opposite side of the car. The fear of what's about to happen next grips you, and your spouse doesn't even cross your mind. Do you know why? Because a third gunman just snatched your three-week-old infant out of the car seat and now is recklessly holding your child. You are now frozen in fear, and the only words that come to your head are, "Please don't hurt my baby."

The gunmen rush you all in the house and straight to the kitchen. Now, your child is crying out to you and your spouse. The baby can feel that the energy is not right. The predator that has your child suddenly does something that almost causes you to pass out. He places your baby in the microwave, turns it on as high as possible, and says, "money, plastic, and jewels right now." He does that to bypass you playing tough or being resistant to what they want. I personally know two different friends who experienced this same scenario. I have another friend that the home invaders killed; the invaders also killed the infant and attempted to kill his wife, but she lived after a gunshot to the head.

I have a childhood friend who was over a friend's house who was spoiled from a financially well-off father. It was five friends having a little get together at the home of the well-off friend's father. What started out as an innocent get-together ended as a bloodbath. All five of them (my friend included) were laid down by four gunmen that invaded the nice home. They put all five people face-down on the floor and shot all of them in the head. My friend was shot in the head and just played dead, hoping the assailants wouldn't shoot him in the head again. Everyone died except him.

There are plenty of women who have been raped by home invaders. Some of the rapists were admirers of the women out in the nightlife or at the job. I know robbers and invaders that went to rob a guy because they felt he had money and ended up raping his wife or girlfriend first because she was cute and with him at the time. There is a guy that I know who is locked up and doing life in prison for selling drugs. Even though I know many of those, I will share a specific story this guy was involved in. For the sake of the story, we will call him Ronnie.

Ronnie had a friend who, once upon a time, was really attracted to this gorgeous female that he used to see out in clubs from time to time. This gorgeous female didn't pay Ronnie's friend any attention. She was in what she considered to be a very serious relationship with a young man who was known for having a lot of money. I won't speculate how he had his small fortune, but he was definitely known for having the window dressing of a street millionaire. Ronnie' s friend would always try to talk to the attractive woman who was involved with the alleged street millionaire; however, the young lady never gave him the time of the day. Ronnie was approached several times by his friend about robbing the alleged street millionaire. For the sake of this story, we'll call the alleged millionaire Chris.

Ronnie realized that his friend really wanted to rob Chris. Neither Ronnie nor his friend knew Chris personally or had ever had any good or bad dealings with him. Nonetheless, it didn't take long before Ronnie caved in and decided to help his friend rob Chris. They started doing their homework on Chris, studying his habits, the cars he drove, etc. The attractive woman Ronnie's friend actually liked lived with Chris.

After Ronnie and his friend gathered all their information on Chris and his girlfriend, they set the date to do the home invasion while they were home. That way, they had a better chance of getting more money or jewelry. You see, most people with large money or jewelry have a good stash spot in the house. Most of the time, that secret stash spot is very difficult to find. Most millionaires keep ten thousand dollars just lying around the house to present to any robbers in the hopes that the robbers will take the ten thousand and go. In actuality, they may have ten times that amount in the house somewhere. Trackers (robbers) that really do they homework will have a pretty good guess if there's more money or jewelry in the house than what's being offered.

Well, on this particular occasion, Ronnie and his friend decided to go rob the home with Chris and his attractive girlfriend there to possibly guarantee them receiving more money from the caper. On the day of the robbery, everything went as Ronnie and his friend planned. Chris and his girlfriend fell right into their routine. The robbers sprung out of the bushes on Chris and his girlfriend just as they had exited the car and in the process of walking up to the house. Ronnie and his friend took Chris and his attractive girlfriend into their house and tied them up. Ronnie smacked Chris around a little bit with his gun and instructed Chris to tell him where the big stash was located. Ronnie walked away from Chris and told his friend to watch Chris and his girlfriend while he went and searched the house.

After about twenty minutes of Ronnie searching the house, he started hearing muffled screams coming from the girlfriend. Ronnie's friend, who was already attracted to the young lady, was supposed to be simply watching them. It alarmed Ronnie because he didn't have any intentions of harming Chris or his girlfriend. He ran downstairs to the floor where he left his friend watching them, hoping that what he was thinking was wrong. Hearing the muffled screams, he figured his friend was raping the girl in front of Chris. The closer he got to where he left them, the more he was convinced that his friend was raping her. Ronnie heard his friend panting, talking, and scuffling. He then ran into the room to see what was going on and he received the shock of his life.

His friend was not raping the attractive girlfriend that he had pursued so many times before. Instead, Ronnie's friend was raping Chris. Ronnie's friend was looking at the attractive girlfriend, but raping her man and saying to her, "Since you never wanted it, I'll give it to your man!"

Ronnie then had to pull himself out of shock and pull his friend— who he now thought was mentally disturbed— off Chris. Due to Ronnie feeling like Chris had just escalated the situation, he told him they needed to kill Chris and his girlfriend. The now rapist totally disagreed. He assured Ronnie that there would be no repercussions for his rapist actions. Thank God, they didn't kill the two, but let me mention something that may be totally irrelevant to the initial reason for sharing this story. A couple of months later, Chris' girlfriend was seen several times in the car with the rapist. Yes, you read that correctly. Ronnie was in shock that his partner in crime actually started dating Chris' girlfriend.

When you decorate yourself with all the bells and whistles of success, foresee the dangers that you inspire. I'm quite sure that a few of you think you're the toughest guy on the planet, and that you can beat up anyone in every situation. Wrong way of thinking! I had a friend who was about six foot three inches with a good size on his bones. He was very flamboyant in his attire and with the vehicles he drove. There was no one who didn't know his name in Columbus, Ohio back then. He could talk a woman into anything in less than two minutes. Street hustlers liked him or hated him, but most respected him. He always told me that he didn't care who it was or how many people it was, he wouldn't allow anyone to rob him at gunpoint. He said that if they pulled a gun on him, they had better be prepared to use it.

One night, about a year before I came to jail, he and I

were about to leave the nightclub when I got a bad feeling. I couldn't identify what I was feeling, but I told my friend to be safe and observant. We parted ways in our ostentatious vehicles, and it wasn't two hours later that I received a page (we had pagers back then) from him with the code "911" displayed. I called him immediately, only to find out that he was in the hospital waiting room.

When I arrived at the hospital, I was greeted by one of his closest friends who took me to where he was. Upon seeing his face, I knew that he was okay. He was smiling from ear to ear with his arm in a sling. He proceeded to explain to me that someone attempted to rob him and the guy who was with them. His version of the events was that two guys with masks and guns ran out from a dark corner when they were walking toward his apartment building (there was a good distance to walk from his apartment parking lot to his apartment door). At gunpoint, the two men ordered my friend and the person with him to go inside his place. My friend refused to comply with the robbers. He purposely created an argument, telling the robbers to do whatever they were going to do right there, and that he would not take them into his home. When he noticed the robber getting slightly distracted, he decided to make a move. He took a step toward the apartment building and suddenly swung a quick punch at the one pointing the gun at him. The robber fell in one direction, and the gun flew in the opposite direction. My friend swung so hard that he lost his balance, fell forward, and ended up dislocating his shoulder, which was why we were at the hospital. The other gunman fled the scene once he saw the fate that had befallen his partner in crime.

My friend was in good spirits as he was clowning his dearest friend who was with him during the robbery. My friend joked, "you might want to check his pants because I know he pissed on himself. He was scared to death. The guys had run off, and his scared ass was standing still with his hands in the air."

After we laughed about the episode, I explained to him and his best friend that they would need to make some changes in order to be safer. I've heard people make up excuses for not having safeguards in their lifestyle habits saying, "anyone can be robbed; you can't stop them if they really want to get you." I totally agree with that, but the key is to "make sure they really want to get you by making it very difficult."

Most people with money or luxurious possessions actually invite robbers with their loose lifestyle, making themselves easy prey for even the most novice robber or home invader. At a minimum, you must protect yourself from the bottom of the criminal pyramid. Notice that a pyramid is wide at the bottom and gets narrow as you move toward the top. If it's an expert or a specialist in robbery or home invasions, they fall toward the top of the pyramid. Those are the ones that I call "trackers." Like I mentioned previously in other writings of mine, there is a difference between "trackers" and jackers.

Jackers capitalize on a moment in time. They see a piece of jewelry, car, or anything they think will be beneficial; they attempt to capitalize on the opportunity. Most don't think of what surprises could spring up, the ability or resources of the potential victim, or how the robbery could go wrong. They just see something and engage on capitalizing on the opportunity.

A tracker is a very dangerous criminal because he or she creates the opportunity to come and get you after they've done their investigations on you. They'll research your habits and the ones of those closest to you. That's to figure out which one has the weakest safeguards. They'll put attractive women or men on you to uncover intimate details about your lifestyle. They'll figure out when you go to get your haircut, where you go, and who does your hair. With all the spy shops they have now, a tracker has access to a lot of tools for use in tracking your movements.

We won't even mention how vast the internet is when it comes to obtaining information on you. For those of you that think the police department will protect you, try this next bit of information on for size: they can't be everywhere all the time, and I've known criminal crews to create diversions on one side of town in order to do something on another. I've seen that happen with people's personal security guards. People create mock fights so a person who appears to be innocuous, who is actually one of the robbers, can get close to the target and snatch the jewelry and run.

To give you a rude awakening, reader, there are plenty of law enforcement officers in prison. There are trackers who actually get their potential targets from dirty cops or compromised members of law enforcement. Basically, you have trackers who will spend five or ten thousand dollars to put together a robbery that might make them hundreds of thousands of dollars. A tracker won't invest that kind of money unless they're sure what's to be gained.

Part of living safe with fame is making sure there are too many unanswered questions about you for a tracker to pick you as a target. Most victims of robberies are being robbed by inexperienced robbers or jackers who think they're trackers. Plainly put, after a jacker builds up his confidence on small things, he'll try bigger ones without really doing his homework. Those people are at the bottom of the robbery pyramid because they don't think and don't have patience. Good safeguards will keep you out of the reach of most of them and will discourage most trackers. Nothing is absolute, though.

Do you know what the ex-factor is to all of this? Someone being upset because you're messing with who they consider their woman or man. Some people will exhaust all resources, all for the thin hope of causing you discomfort when it comes to matters of the heart. When I was in the height of my drug dealing career, I would not mess with another big drug dealer's woman or mother of his children. I would always tell guys that were in the drug trade, "you already have enough open enemies. You do not need to add a motivated enemy to that list." I understand the territorial mindset of any male species. There are a lot of people who are in very bad situations and have no clue that a jilted lover or a lover's ex-mate did it to them.

My friend who dislocated his shoulder while foiling the robber's plans outside of his apartment is now dead. Three years after I was incarcerated, I received a letter that my friend had been murdered. According to the newspaper, it was a robbery. A large quantity of cocaine was found at the scene; they believed someone called him for the packages but shot him when he wouldn't hand them over. I have another friend that I grew up with in elementary school in Dayton, Ohio. He was at a carnival one day with a very expensive gold rope around his neck, one that resembled the large gold-roped chains that many rappers wore back in the late 1980's. Someone walked up behind him, snatched his chain, and took off running. My friend took off running right behind him and when my friend started getting too close, the guy turned around and shot him in the head.

I have way more horrific stories about robberies and home invasions than I care to mention. I only hope you don't categorize these situations as being those of victims being in a life of crime. You see, that would be far from the truth. From all walks of life, people get robbed at gunpoint every day for all sorts of things. I have an Aunt Ruth who lives in Detroit and is a very accomplished career woman. She's worked for General Motors all her adult life and possesses a couple of degrees. My aunt was robbed at gunpoint while coming out of her apartment with a few female friends. They were all headed on a girl's night out. At the time, my aunt drove a very nice aqua-colored Seville Cadillac. However, most people who lived around her were not so fortunate. The robber took over a hundred thousand dollars of jewelry off my aunt. She had acquired very exquisite pieces of jewelry from hard work and dedication in her career. The ironic part is, one of the women with my aunt that night was a Detroit police officer who was armed. The robber got the drop on them, meaning that he had his gun out with the element of surprise. There was nothing that my aunt's best friend could do. She danced around the car and wouldn't stay still as the robber requested.

Once the robber had relieved my aunt of her jewelry and began to flee; her friend pursued him, and shots were fired— to no avail, though. He made off with all her jewels, but I was glad that he didn't make off with her life. Her friend did the right thing. To this day, my aunt still drives brand new Cadillac vehicles, but she does not wear expensive jewelry in large volumes. I don't even think she even owns a hundred thousand dollars' worth of jewels anymore. My aunt was robbed for that amount of jewelry back in the mid 80's. It was a very traumatic experience for her. She lived through it, but she learned.

Individuals who have never been through that ordeal or witnessed it don't really believe that it will happen to them. That kind of thinking can cost you your life.

In my opinion, my aunt should've seen the suspicious person from afar, but how does a person believe that can happen to a person that it hasn't happened to? Hindsight is always 20/20, though. Her friend, the police officer, did notice the peculiar movements of someone, which allowed her to sidestep the line of fire of the robber. However, she didn't want to do anything to endanger my aunt. My point is that her friend spotted the guy because she had police training. When you reach certain lifestyles, you must be trained to see certain things.

I've seen so much and know of so much loss of life and material possessions. I don't believe most law enforcement know what most conscious major drug dealers know about safety. I offer advice and counseling on lifestyle changes because I know that what you don't know about fame will hurt you. Let me make my point very clear as to why I'm highlighting this. First and foremost, it is only by the grace of God that I haven't been robbed or hurt while in the thickness of my large drug deals. I had a lot of safeguards and tricks in my activities in order to protect myself and those with me. I just want you to know, reader, that I know my level of consciousness in protecting myself is secondary to my divine shield of protection.

Even my deeper depths of wisdom about safeguards

come from an omnipotent source of wisdom. A lot of people have experienced what I have and possibly more but have failed to capture and apply the wisdom that I have from those experiences. I am extremely grateful to be able to discover, diagnose, develop, and deliver knowledge the way I do. To demonstrate the different levels of training and abilities to process information, I will explain something that took place at my trials.

At trial, one of the detectives that was investigating me before I was arrested mentioned how I was very aware of any kind of surveillance. Detective Wilson gave detailed accounts of how I foiled their attempts to follow me time and time again. The officers tried using three or four different vehicles to follow me, basically letting one car follow me so far and then having that officer turn off, then letting the officer behind him go a distance with me before he turned off to allow another one to follow me. This was done all in the hopes of disguising their surveillance techniques. When I would catch on to their tactics, I would simply pull over on the side of the road, get out of the car and watch all of them go by. My flamboyant vehicle would never go to my home; I left it in a twenty-four-hour storage area. One day, I'm quite sure Detective Wilson was deathly scared. I was only about two blocks from my home when I noticed a car pull out of a parking lot and get behind me. Of course, I had just what the doctor ordered. I pulled up in a driveway of a home that wasn't my residence and acted like I was fiddling with my keys to unlock the door, giving the impression that it was my residence. Just as expected, the car that was some ways back sped up into the affluent community. That let me know that the driver was speeding up to see what place I was going into. As soon as the car passed me and turned the corner, I jumped back in my truck and followed him. At the time, I didn't know who was following me or if he was actually tailing me. My instincts were telling me that he was. I indiscreetly tailed the car from a very safe distance. The car went into a strip mall parking lot that was closed. It was just a little past midnight, and that was a major indicator to me that the car was definitely law enforcement. I could now see that the driver was a middle-aged white male. Him being law enforcement was obvious to me because he pulled up into a commercial property after hours in Dublin, Ohio, which was and still is one of the more affluent communities on the outskirts of Columbus, Ohio. What he did next confirmed my intuitions.

He parked next to a building, turned on his interior light, and started writing as if he was jotting down notes. His arrogance or comfort astonished me. He never looked up for one moment. He never suspected that the watcher could be the watched, that the follower could become the followed. Watching him, I adopted a lesson that I would adhere to for the rest of my life. No matter what level, status, ranking, or position that I may hold in life, I would never assume that I could not become the victim of someone appearing to be less resourceful from a lower vantage point.

The will of an individual may instantly make him or her an overcomer of any obstacle in getting to you. Absolutely no one is totally untouchable. That night, Detective Wilson came face to face with that reality. After I realized that it was probably law enforcement following me, I decided to let him know that I knew. Just in case it was a tracker following me, he would shut down his plans or be discouraged from being exposed. I parked and watched him from the entrance of the mall parking lot. I positioned myself directly across from the entrance, wanting to make sure that when he began to pull out of the lot, his lights would shine directly at my driver's side window. For shock value, I looked directly into the lights of his car as he exited. I could tell that it frightened him because his brake lights came on, then as he was turning out of the lot, our vehicles were parallel as we made eye contact. I gave him a sly respectful grin, and he looked shocked and frightened. .

During my three-week trial, he testified that he had never experienced those counter surveillance situations before. He gave accounts of several situations when they attempted to trail me, but their plans were destroyed by things I had done, after which they were unable to set back up because the measures I had taken made it too difficult. I'm in no way attempting to glorify myself for the sake of making this chapter assist this book in being a national bestseller. My intention is to aid the ordinary person that is achieving in extraordinary fashion, to understand some of the elements that go along with being a standout.

I've always taken things a lot more serious than most. I've realized that so many people learn on different levels in their own way. Nonetheless, a person might have instant wealth or success, but may not have the luxury of an adjustment period to develop safeguards for fame. Having your license plates linked to your present residence can prove detrimental to your safety. Giving your home phone number out can be hazardous for your life. Knowing where to get a hotel room and the position of the room is essential for safety. For most people, putting more money in their hands or giving them fame brings more grief and pain.

About ten years ago, a certain martial artist actor was reported on the news as being extorted by gangsters. Yes, movie stars and entertainers are being extorted by the truckload. Some are receiving the soft press or the "tender lean" as I call it. That's the extortion shallowly camouflaged under the umbrella of a friendship. Then, it's the blunt "in your face" extortion that flat out threatens you and or your family's lives. At the very least, the extortioners disrupt or threaten the fluidity of your business, stating that if they can't get some of your money, then you won't make any money. There are a few different ways to handle that. Nonetheless, this isn't the book for all the solutions. This is simply the chapter for pointing out a few of the problems that come with success.

In mentoring some of the most gorgeous and talented young ladies I've ever seen, I've had to advise them on image safety. There are so many people that have money to burn or two-way mirrors, spy cameras, and hidden microphones. It is so easy to have naked pictures of an up and coming young actress or entertainer. Blackmail is also a very nasty game that is played with people that have money or fame. Sometimes, beautiful young ladies are filmed or recorded without their knowledge strictly for entertainment. People with money just pass the pictures or videos around to one other. People have two-way mirrors in their bathrooms of their million-dollar homes. To make this all clear, I will do a brief recap.

You may have individuals that will get compromising material on you in order to blackmail you. However, you may have individuals that have plenty of money who just want naked pictures, video footage, or taped conversations of you, strictly to share with the boys or girls for entertainment while having a beer. Material like that often leaks out eventually.

I've never done it personally, but I've noticed people with plenty of money who have spent a hundred thousand dollars and more for hidden cameras. They used these cameras for no other reason than to film women in vulnerable situations, while in these guy's home. Being around people who have money to spend on expensive toys or gadgets is a whole new arena that most women are not ready for. There is an old saying that states you can tell a lot about a person by what he or she produces. I then add to that and say that by what a person produces, he or she must be blindly prepared. By whatsoever a person may produce, that same product may cause them to be reduced. A so-called life enhancement may not necessarily be a personal one.

THE CRYSTALLIZING (GOAL WRITING)

This chapter was actually written last, but I allowed my instincts to guide me to place it before the last chapter. What is it that drives people to keep priceless information from the multitudes that could positively change lives? I guess I'll never figure out that part of life, but then again, I guess that's not my job. I believe my job is to manifest and reveal. I've learned that one of the best kept secrets amongst successful people is "Goal Writing."

We often hear or read a lot about focus, visualizing, verbalizing, and internalizing. Yet, the true spark plug to bringing any goal into fruition is written word. There is a precise way that the word must be written. You must first become what you want to see. The key to manifest writing is to write in order to get or receive. Whatever you seek to have or achieve is just a thought. It is not yet in the physical realm. Most of the people who want things are not very clear with themselves as to what they want, so how could the universe ever be clear as to what to manifest?

Something as simple as writing your goals down as if you already have them is one of the world's best kept secrets. When you write your goals down and date them, you bring a thought energy into a physical realm's energy. The minute you write it and date it, the goal has then been birthed into the physical reality. Clarity brings crystallizing   from verbalizing, visualizing, and

internalizing. The written word goes all the way back beyond biblical days.

If you reflect back on the Bible stories, you can see this truth all through them. Moses received the written word on tablets or stones form the burning bush. What astonished me is how most ministers teach over and around the book of Habakkuk in the Bible. Habakkuk 2: 2—3 says "And the Lord answered me, and said, write the vision and make it plain on tablets so that they may run with it that hastens by. For the vision is yet for an appointed time, but at the end it shall speak, and not lie; though it tarry, wait for it; because it will surely come, it will not tarry."

When I was writing this book, I thought this book was complete when I finished the chapter, "Train Your Replacement." Nonetheless, I know that nothing is truly complete or finished until your spirit says so. Therefore, after writing what I thought was the last chapter, I sat still in spirit, basically waiting and listening to that still small voice inside to truly know that I was done. It didn't take long before I was bubbling over inside with the written word. Another chapter (this one) had to be written. Of course, I called my mother and told her that I felt like I needed to write another chapter. Upon explaining my intuition, insight, and instincts about writing this chapter to her, she directed me to the book of Habakkuk. She confirmed my decision to write this chapter and the information that I planned to divulge in it.

There are countless talks of studies on students in college writing their goals versus the ones who don't. The results were alleged to be amazing regarding the high success rate of the students who wrote their goals down. Most of the time, we are getting exactly what we asked for, even though it's not what we want. Try stitching or knitting a piece of clothing without precise size, measurement, and design. It will not come out right. There has to be a pattern or a clear mold as to what the finished product looks like. Millions of people ask for things with more confusion and unsureness than clarity.

Do you know how many women in the world say, "I want a good man?" Others think that they are being a lot clearer when they say, "I don't care what he looks like, but I want a good man."

Well, what does a good man look like to the universe? What does good look like? Does that mean he has good intentions, but he beats women? Maybe it means that he doesn't beat women, but he's lazy. He can be a good man and lazy. He can be a good man but prefer not to bathe. He can be a good man, but lack patience or tolerance for your family's shortcomings.

To the men, what's a good woman? The same goes on both sides. Sometimes, two good people can't be in a relationship together. Therefore, you can get that good man or woman and still not have anything worth having in the relationship aspect. The relationship skills have to match up and have the potential to enhance and compliment each other. That information is for another book.

The point is very simple, though. What does good look like to the universe? Good is what you say it is for you. It is relative to the individual. What you deem good qualities may be average or weak qualities for the next individual. You must identify exactly what "good" looks like for you. If not, you're getting what you asked for, yet it may still not be what you want. That's like praying, meditating, or asking for a really nice sweater. What is a nice sweater for you?

Picture what happens when two people are married or simply live together, but there is no clarity in wants and desires. You have misdirected energy that simply fizzles out. It accomplishes nothing. Once the thrills of living together or whatever newness inspired the union wears thin, the relationship struggles. A couple must work out exactly what will make them both happy. What if both people are praying for a nice house, however, one's version of a nice house is one close to the city for easy travels to the stores; that person wants a house that the couple could work on together. However, the other person's idea of a nice home is one they had to do very little work to and was far away from the city. Now, both of these pictures of a nice home are totally different and neither has written a detailed word of what their nice home really looked like. They would need to be in agreement and then write the "nice" down.

Our energies help create our realities; if there is a couple with divided energies, then nothing can come from that. They are fighting each other's energy. When two or more people come together in alignment of thought and written word, you have a movement of collective consciousness. It's a lot easier to acquire things when two people are working toward the same goals, or at least are clear in helping each other go after their goals. You may write short-term goals that take place in a couple of weeks, and long-term goals that come about within two years.

I've found that it is critical to get over the fear of setting a goal not having it come to pass by the prescribed date. The only way to do that is to simply get to it. Start writing down goals and dates to get to your manifesting. From one accomplishment to the next, you'll get more confident in manifesting. Think of an easy goal that you would like to obtain in the near future. Be clear and precise. Next, put the date next to it when it will appear in your life. Be very specific and always write in the present, as if you already have whatever you're seeking. Write "have such and such." I can't stress enough to be very clear about the goal and what nice and good are for you. Put the date down that you've written the goal on, and then the date that it is to be achieved on.

If the goal doesn't manifest for you by that date, do not get discouraged. It could that be something is wrong with the goal, or you could be blocking your blessing. Look at the goal you wrote closely and rewrite it with a new date. Always remember that people and circumstances will appear in order to help manifest these goals. Expect everything that confronts you to have the potential to possibly provide an important element to materialize your goals.

When I originally started selling drugs, I bought a GMC Astro Minivan. I had it painted a pretty blue with chrome sparkle flakes in the paint. On the sides of the minivan, I had chrome panels put on that read, "MADE IT." Now, what no one realized back then was that the words were from a gospel poem I had written entitled *I MADE IT* at twelve or thirteen years old. When I wrote the words below, I had to sit down with a pen and yes, it took me all night. I distributed my feelings, wrote them down on paper, and wanted to go around the world just like the equator.

I MADE IT.

I didn't think I would make it. I thought it was a myth.

I didn't know God would give me such a talented gift.

You see, I wanted to work, but didn't want to slave

So, I got down on my knees and I started to pray.

I said, "Sir, please give me talent, my heart is torn."

He said, "But son, I gave you talent when you were born.

I said, "But sir, I lost my talent and I just can't cope.

He said, "You never lost your talent, you just lost your hope."

He said, "Go rap to the world because with Him, you're safe and you'll never lose your talent if you keep His faith.

That's why I MADE IT.

If you're cold in the winter, he can be your

cover.

If you need parental guidance, he can be your mother.

If you're hot in the summer, he can be your fan.

If you're sick lying in bed, he's the medicine man.

Compliments I received, Creative Rapper I achieved.

I'm really being blessed because it's Him that I believe.

I MADE IT.

I can see my brother killed, hear my mother scream.

He can touch me on my head and make it all a dream.

Me and God are close like a root and tree.

My name is Charles Dunn, but you can call me Chuck Dee.

Instead of going to a shack and buying some crack

I went and brought a pen and pad to form this rap.

That's why

I MADE IT.

Now, let me tell you some very interesting points. Number one is that the original poem ended at the lines of, ""my name is Charles Dunn, but you can call me Chuck Dee." Then, a crack epidemic came out when I was very young in high school, and I added the last verse about the crack. The second point is that I never wanted to be a rapper, yet I said I was a rapper in that poem. However, I am a speaker and receive enormous amounts of compliments from people all over the world for my speeches and poetry (which I'm very thankful to God for).

Lastly, but certainly not least, I was claiming that I had MADE IT, but hadn't been through anything. The mindset that I could experience the loss, of my biggest hero's (my brother) NFL career, but that God could touch me and make it all a dream shared my level of spirituality. What I'm basically sharing with you, the reader, is that I wrote about victories as a child before the wars or challenges really began. That was my written word. I wrote about going to rap or speak to the people when no one was really listening to me and there were really no people to talk to, nor did I really have much to say.

There is so much that can be examined by things that I wrote as a child and how they relate today. I can't remember the whole song I wrote, but I remember this much. The song was called *Dwill You*, meaning do you do these things and if you don't, will you?

> *Do you feel? Do you love? Do you cry? Do you share? When you see a person crying, do you stop? Do you care?*

Do you love?

When you see the blue waters and the sun is bright,

Do you think about the people that have no sight?

Do you care?

End.

Of course, there was more to that song than that, but you get the point. That was written when I was about sixteen. Now, let's fast forward to when I first got convicted and received a thirty-year sentence after I lost at trial. Still in the county jail and not knowing what real prison was going to be like, I wrote a very powerful poem called *Going the Distance*. Many of my females and male friends had abandoned me, not including some family that had turned their backs in shame. Examine just the title *Going the Distance*. That's not a statement of maybe, hopefully, or doubting. That's a commanding statement from a twenty-three year old young man about to encounter the most life threatening experience of his existence, yet he has no idea of the levels of dangers that he will face. This is the poem that I wrote:

Distance is defined as something in time or space.

It doesn't matter how fast or slow, as long as you keep up the pace.

Going the distance is power generated by a force.

Neither one can be obtained unless one recognizes the source,

If one would keep thoughts infinite and look through all the illusions.

Going the distance in life wouldn't be such a mass confusion.

When you're thinking of the past and all the good things that suit ya

It could never hold a light to the dreams of the future.

Tears are in my heart and the pain is still groovin'.

But I believe in myself and I gotta keep on movin'.

Though pain and sorrow go hand in hand, I'm willing to die like Martin Luther King in the Promised Land.

People turned their backs on me, but they said I was so good.

They never went the distance, but they said they did the best they could.

You forgot about me and left me to die.

You said I was never coming home.

When you pass me in the street

Don't think it was a clone.

You expect those to go the distance

With whom you have an emotional bond

Some can run the two-hundred-yard dash

But aren't prepared for the marathon.

For those who made up excuses

Like I sprained my ankle or I lost my shoe.

I hope when it's time for you to go the distance

That someone's there for you.

End

These two written works can be interpreted as written declarations or even mantras. However it's viewed, it was written that I would make it, and that I would persevere. Not knowing the end from the beginning is how most feel, but why not know the end? You have the power to do so. My mother once told me that someone could leave an inheritance of a million dollars to someone. Nonetheless, they can't receive it if they don't go sign for it and claim it. We too have an inheritance. It's a spiritual inheritance that belongs to us, but we never go sign for it and claim it.

I look at how Muhammed Ali would always write, speak, chant (in poem), and claim when he would defeat his opponents in the boxing ring. Back then, some people thought he was too arrogant. Others thought he was charming, witty, or funny. He would always coin himself as "The Greatest of All Time," He spoke in riddles, rhymes, or poetry. "Float like a butterfly, sting like a bee, (whomever) is going down in three. Muhammed Ali claimed his victories in written word. He told the world that he was the greatest of all time. He claimed that inheritance to the point that when he no longer said it, we the people started saying it about him. Even today, when we use the term "the greatest of all time," most people think of him.

Tons of people have asked me why I didn't lose my mind going through my ordeal. Well, my mind wasn't mine to lose. Once your spirit clicks into this formula for success, auto pilot takes over. If you're looking at your situation in the world through carnal eyes, then you may be totally lost. If you're beginning to examine your world through spiritual eyes, then you grasp these concepts.

In crystallizing your goals, being able to repeat them aloud in some manner also empowers the manifestation. Subconsciously, I knew the process of true manifestation. Writing my goals in poem, to be spoken repeatedly, was innately deep within. I actually had to catch up in wisdom today what I naturally knew as a child and young adult from yesterday. The adult poems that I've written long before I wrote this book are *You Created It* and *Built to Last*. I hope your journey brings you to collide with mine at a point when I am performing one or both of these poems. In life, we end up being confronted with what we're ready for.

At the point of receiving that result, we should be

writing the next page of our book of life. We are the authors of our future. This exists if we choose to write it or get swept away in whatever comes because we didn't write it.

TRAINING YOUR REPLACEMENT

We live in a society in which the word *replacement* has had a somewhat bad reputation; not all the time, but it has been generally used when something has happened to the original. This closing chapter is to the contrary of what you just read. You need to train your replacement so that other things can and will happen to you. People generally fear being replaced, therefore keeping so many things secretive that others around them are stagnated. Thus, making everyone dependent upon them.

When you truly can't be denied, you are forced into perpetual greatness from aligned efforts and unseen forces. When you hold valuable information from someone who potentially deserves it and will walk in it, then you are holding yourself back as well. You need to train your replacement for so many reasons.

From a personal achievement level, often times, a position comes with unseen sticky circumstance, meaning that most people get stuck in that particular position. They may whine, complain, and moan about not climbing the corporate ladder while in reality, they are not pushing themselves to the next level. Training your replacement will not limit you; it will boost you to the next plateau. When you've trained your replacement, you will be breaking into a higher level of your own development. The trainee has their own identity and will follow your structure but will apply those principles differently. No matter what you teach me and how you teach me to do it, it will be done slightly different. That slight alteration will create innovation. How the surroundings respond to the slight difference may convert underachieving into overachieving in another individual. One thing that it will do is force you into a new space to discover, develop, design, and explore uncharted territory.

I once read somewhere that true success requires successors. After all your hard work, the gathering of connections, the implementation of divine guidance, all the way to the conquering of your goals, what's next? Train your replacement. Pass along that formula and transfer the knowledge that ignites the increase in one's life.

I have a friend who worked for a major security firm in Tampa, Florida. He was very proficient at his job and his employer loved him. He knew everyone's job, and his presence made everything go smoothly at the company. When a supervisor position came open at the job, my friend thought he was sure to get it. My friend shared with me how he was so effective at his job. He had developed ways of making the customers feel extra safe. His customer service was also well beyond the standards of the company. My friend was passed over for the promotion, and he was definitely shocked and heartbroken. Another position came open at the company he worked for about thirteen months after he was passed over for the first one. He was passed over for the second promotion as well.

Basically discouraged and leaning toward quitting his job, he wanted to ask his employer for a sit-down. He wanted to humbly ask him what it was he needed to work on in order to avoid being passed up for anymore promotions. When he finally got ahold of his ego and emotions, he had that meeting with his employer. My friend didn't anticipate what his employer told him.

There was one thing that he did to strengthen his position. That was surprising to him because he always felt that he knew everything better than the owner did about operating the business. What the owner told him was that no one knew how to do what he did. The owner explained to him that he never passed along his tricks for successful daily operations. Him holding back the knowledge of his great results also held him back in his position. "Train your replacement naturally without receiving a promotion, and then I'll see about you getting one," is what the employer told him. That comment from his employer may sound confusing. Let me explain.

When you train a replacement to do your job without you actually having another job, you'll do it in detail. You will be patient and be able to work with the individual in harmony. Having another job or space to occupy will actually occupy space in your mind and heart. most of the time, it will divide your mental energies. Not to mention that you will be on some type of a timetable, basically transitioning into your new post and out of your old one. Your employer really won't have the opportunity to see how your replacement impacts the company. By the time he finds out whatever he finds out, it won't matter because you're promoted on. He has to work with it as is.

Training your replacement is so important in so many areas. In order to get more of something, you must be willing to give something away. This is on a spiritual level. Knowledge is really not yours to hoard any way. It belongs to a source of plenty. Share what you perceive is yours and you'll receive more. Lead, and then receive. Generate, and then turn to others to educate so they may emulate, and you will in turn elevate.

When I was incarcerated in Ohio, I taught a lot of classes and always found myself speaking in front of large crowds at the prison. It was always a graduation ceremony, poetry slam, or a religious setting. Whatever the case, the warden of the institution passed a directive on to the staff to ban me from speaking. One of the officers told me that the warden was really concerned about my influence on his compound. The warden felt that his compound was really my compound whenever I got ready for it to be. He did not want one inmate to have as much power as I had at his facility. He mentioned that he didn't care how much positivity that I had saturated the prison population with. There was just too much of a disparity between the average inmate and Charles Dunn in his mind.

The beautiful thing about it was I had been mentoring a young man from Brooklyn, New York who was incarcerated at the facility. His name is Herman Baron. He had become my assistant in every class that I taught and had started teaching his own classes at the prison. He heard me perform poetry and fell in love with the art of poetry. I passed on every ounce of wisdom or guidance as any situation required. Unbeknownst to me, I was training my replacement. From my classes, he was inspired and started teaching an urban studies class. I learned a lot from his class. Little did I know that I would learn much more. I was transitioning and didn't even know it. My intent was merely to give that young man as much of myself as he could use, in the hopes of him making greater connections within himself.

I had spent almost ten years in that one prison when I was banned from speaking in front of the population. Everyone would always tell me that everyone would be at a great loss when I left that prison. Every prisoner at the facility was assigned a case manager. A case manager was an officer who oversaw your case file. You are able to go to that person with any issues with your security levels, programming, release date, etc. No one knows your criminal charges and what happened on your case better than your case manager. It's their job to know about your institutional adjustment and the particulars of your case. Well, my first case manager at that facility told me that I better get comfortable because due to the severity of my charges, I would never go to a federal prison camp. A camp is a minimum-security institution where there are no officers assigned to your housing units, and usually, the doors stay open all night. A prison camp is the lowest security level of prison. The only thing better than that is being released or possibly going to the halfway house, which is still in the community.

Now, there I was, stuck (according to my case manager) in a low facility prison, and I felt like I was being limited as to what I could do there. I would like you, the reader, to make another mental note (I mentioned it earlier in this book) that I wrote this book—while at the federal prison camp that the case manager told me I would never get to. Even though I had been silenced from speaking in front of large groups, I had already trained my replacement. The young man, Herman Baron, took the reins and rode it like the champion he is.

As I've mentioned previously in my material, everything in existence must justify its existence. When it no longer does, it begins the process of being removed from existence. Purposeful things and people will never sit by idling too long while others ignore their presence.

My existence could no longer be justified at that low security prison that I was being housed at. Thus, I had to be removed to occupy another space for another purpose. Elements lined up, and the magic happened. Thank God for the deliverance.

I had trained my replacement, and I could no longer be held in that time and space. I had to move on, or the universe moved me on. Whichever way it happened, I had to leave there. I believe that life works just like that. Resist selfish motives and respond to your success with gratitude and observation. Be on the lookout for your replacement. Shatter the fears and realize that training your replacement is stretching you into another dimension. You solve and simplify problems when you pass on creative tools to a fresh view (your replacement). Do you just expect to take, receive, and retain your entire life? You must give it away to get it.

Take a few moments and ask yourself what were the great messengers from yesteryear doing? When you undress their work in human development, you will see that they were training their replacement. What are you doing when you transfer the best parts of yourself to your children by teaching them how to provide and care for their brothers and sisters? When we enhance our cultures, communities, and our nation, we are training our replacements to refresh our world.

The perpetuation of life is a product of trained replacements increasing the quality of our living. It's unthinkable to the carnal individual because they can't see beyond self, but every time an individual is replaced by their trainee, their accomplishments become timeless. You never fail because you're always being added to. Jesus made mention of this accomplishment theory when he stated that, "man shall do what he's done and greater works they shall accomplish."

I'm training as many worthy replacements as I can that show up with an inspired mind and a genuine heart. The cells in your body even replace themselves. You have cells training their replacements. I will not be denied because our forefathers said that if I followed the steps in this book that I wouldn't be, and I haven't been. I am a trained replacement of some of the greatest energies that have ever walked under our sun. They were not denied in anything. From civil rights, avionics, and famine lands to transforming ignorance and foolishness and the wisdom of sages. I am birthed out of the impossible. One of my father's nicknames is Mr. Unbelievable; I am his messenger's trained replacement. My trainers are conquerors and overcomers. I've been trained to be humble, but to penetrate the illusionary force fields of this world. I've been trained to always stay on the road of self-mastery. Succeeding is not a thing to be done, yet a thing to be recognized. I realized that I must help you, the reader, realize that every great individual you've ever read about or heard about, you are their replacement. So, how do you take all that power and DNA, just to make mediocre or (even worse) nothing of yourself? The only reason why you are denied in life is because you believe you can be.

ABOUT THE AUTHOR

Charles "Silk Dunn" is a national icon, a global life coach and motivational speaker whose passion is to empower the movement of the masses in their evolution toward peace, power, and happiness.

Dunn was sentenced to a 30 year imprisonment at the age of 23. During this time, he was featured in the Southeast Alabama Gazette Newspaper as America's Mandela. Mr. Dunn has taught tens of thousands of federal prisoners as well as life coached numerous celebrities. His self-development courses had a waiting list of at least a year.

While incarcerated, Dunn was carefully executing a process of discovery and self-improvement. He received over 100 certifications, and created curriculums for five different programs, ranging from anger management to mental wellness. In addition, he designed a Mental Wellness class which combines, mind, body, spirit, and universe. Released from prison on November 1, 2015, Dunn has spoken at several public schools in the Metro Atlanta Area.

Mr. Dunn continues to blaze a trail of power and progress fueled by hard work and positive energy. Often known as the uncommon mentor, Dunn may be small in stature but he is mighty in impact. His ability to exchange tragedy for triumph makes him one of the most inspiring figures in the country.

Made in the USA
Columbia, SC
18 January 2019